How Savvy W
Get Promoted, Get

YOUR
POWER
UNLEASHED

Creator of the DIVA Method ®
KISHA WYNTER

Design and distribution by Bublish
Published by Bublish, Inc.
ISBN: 978-1-647048-30-3 (paperback)
ISBN: 978-1-647048-32-7 (hardcover)
ISBN: 978-1-647048-29-7 (eBook)
ISBN: 978-1-647048-31-0 (audiobook)

Contents

Foreword

By Lisa Nichols

In the heart of South-Central Los Angeles, where I was raised, the concept of living anything other than a paycheck-to-paycheck existence seemed like a distant dream. For the initial twenty-eight years of my life, every move I made in my career was driven by the urgent need for that next paycheck. Landing a job was never the challenge for me; I had a knack for communication, making me a favorable candidate in interviews. The real struggle was in keeping those jobs. At twenty-five after being let go from my fourth job in five years, I found myself aimlessly browsing job listings, three months unemployed, behind on rent, and without my car that had just been repossessed. Despite the urgency of my situation, I felt paralyzed, unable to take the next step. These events brought me to my knees forcing me to dig deep and ask myself some powerful questions regarding what I really wanted from life. To my surprise, the answers flowed with ease: I yearned to explore the world, to make a meaningful difference in the lives of others, to don a sleek black business suit, and to wield a laptop as my tool.

This epiphany marked a turning point in my career. No longer was I in pursuit of mere financial survival; I sought work that resonated with my soul. My approach to job searching changed; I evaluated potential employers as much as they assessed me. Soon, I joined a computer software company that aligned with my new-found aspirations, offering me the chance to travel, assist others through training, and yes, even wear that coveted black business suit and carry a laptop. The role evolved to allow me to focus on what ignited my soul—motivating others—eventually leading me to my life's calling with my company Motivating the Masses.

Your Power Unleashed: How Savvy Women Use Courage to Get Promoted, Get Paid, and Find Fulfillment by Kisha Wynter is the EXACT tool that I needed in my life. A resource that will inspire and equip you to breakthrough your own personal and professional barriers. Notice that I didn't say just your work life, because how we do one thing is how we do everything. When we are free from the limits in one area, that freedom reigns in all other areas. Kisha, a kindred spirit and warrior in her own right, lays out a blueprint for women to navigate the office to the outdoors with courage, conviction, and a profound sense of purpose.

As I reflect on my own path, from the depths of despair in my small apartment in Los Angeles to reaching heights I once thought unattainable, I see a reflection of the process Kisha proposes. It is a path paved with the courage to confront and transform your inner critic into your inner coach, to align your career with your core values, and to embrace the audacity to take an unwavering stance for what you are worth, even when it feels like no one is standing with you. It's about shifting from a place of seeking external validation to cultivating an unshakeable confidence within.

Your Power Unleashed is more than just a guide for career advancement; it's a manifesto for living a life imbued with purposeful power. Kisha shepherds you through the process of turning self-doubt into self-assurance, fear into boldness, and dreams into reality. She provides a clear roadmap to those who are ready to step into their greatness but may not know where to start.

My hope for you, as you turn the pages of this book, is that you will feel seen, understood, and empowered. May you realize that the power to change your circumstances, to ascend in your career, and to live a life filled with joy and fulfillment, has not only been your birth right but has always been right at your fingertips. The journey may require you to confront your fears, to step outside of your comfort zone, and to shake up unjust systems, but I assure you, it is worth every step.

As you embark on this transformative adventure, know that you are not alone. There is a community of women, myself included, who are walking this path with you, cheering you on every step of the way. Together, let us rise, let us unleash our power, and let us create a world where every woman has the courage and the opportunity to live out her wildest dreams.

Your sister in prosperity and possibility,
Lisa Nichols

Introduction

"Yes, she's smart—a strategic thinker who sees around corners and consistently delivers results. She's a strong leader of her team and goes above and beyond expectations in her role. You can depend on her to come through every time because this woman has an unbelievable work ethic, and everyone likes her—from her team to her clients to her peers to her managers. But there's just one thing missing."

This is an excerpt from yet another performance review discussion that I was a part of as a human resources leader, working for one of the most prestigious leadership development programs at an esteemed Fortune 500 company. The manager was presenting his case on how strong of a performer his female team leader was and was about to give his final verdict on whether she was ready to be promoted.

I waited for it, and I knew exactly what he was going to say to his peers (other middle managers): "She has everything it takes to be promoted, but she's missing just one thing—confidence. She doesn't speak with the level of authority that will get respect from leaders. She shies away from difficult conversations. She doesn't speak up when certain senior executives are in the room. She's basically a wallflower."

Wallflower is the kiss of death in the career of any ambitious woman in the corporate world.

In my twenty years as a corporate HR leader—and now as a leadership development consultant and executive coach—I cannot tell you how many times I've heard some version of this statement. The smart, diligent, strong female who has all the hard skills that it takes to advance to the next level of her leadership journey—except for confidence, executive presence, influence, or some other "must have" that's only a sugarcoated way of saying that she lacks the ability to show up in her power and own the room.

On this particular day, in this particular discussion, I'd had enough. Enough of hearing how a brilliant woman was living below her potential. Enough of the leaders who she worked with misdiagnosing the root cause of her timidity as if they were psychologists. Enough of her worth being summed up and discredited by one overly simplistic phrase—*lack of confidence*. Enough of being told to go and "fix her"—as if she were broken.

There was a huge disconnect. And on that day, at that moment, I decided that if anyone was going to stand in the gap, it clearly had to be me. Not because I had some magical superpower to fix anyone, but because I didn't believe these women were broken. In fact, it was the *system* that was broken. But I had to be the one to take a stand for three reasons.

One, I was lucky enough in my role as an HR leader to be one of the few who was in these behind-the-scenes conversations on a regular basis. I recognized that most people in the corporate workplace are not usually exposed to what's being said about top talent behind closed doors, so they wouldn't know how to coach these women to help them win at work.

Two, I'm a woman in the corporate space who's had to figure out for herself how to own her power. As a female who came up in corporate America, I was told in a hundred ways by male leaders to be more confident—that I needed to be bolder, to walk in with a swagger as if I owned the room, and on and on. To be fair to them, the men who gave this advice were very well intentioned, and they believed in me. But I knew if I swung the pendulum too far, I would be penalized. If I didn't walk that *confidence* or *power* tightrope very carefully as a woman, it wouldn't be long before I would be called bitchy and suffer the repercussions of this career-limiting label.

Moreover, being a Black woman, I might also be called angry behind my back—or even, on a few rare occasions, to my face. I will save the story of the leader who was brazen enough to say this directly to me for another time. I had to figure out how to build my own confidence and overcome self-doubt, fear, and internal criticism in a place that didn't get me. This is what I recognized and heard on the call that day. These leaders didn't understand women—not because they didn't care (I believe many of them really did), but because they'd never walked a mile in our shoes. And we, as females, are socialized in a world that isn't exactly nurturing to the leadership potential of little girls. Now, as grown women, we are expected to powerfully own the room at work—but just be careful not to own it *too much*!

The third reason was that I was finally frustrated enough to do something about it. I was frustrated because the leaders didn't get it, and their advice was, absolute rubbish! I was frustrated because these women were brilliant and could literally transform the workplace if they only had the audacity to see their own glory and operate in it. I was frustrated because the system and environment in which they worked weren't designed for them to win.

This was the pain I felt, seeing women not live the fulfilling professional lives they were destined to live—lives of contribution, impact, and purpose. I've learned that wherever your pain is, that's where your purpose lies. By leaning into the purpose despite the pain, you receive the power to break through. I identified with these women because, early in my career, I *was* them. Now, every time I enter a brand-new space that I'm not familiar with, which stretches me outside of my comfort zone, I'm reminded of that pain. The work that I've been doing with women over the past eleven-plus years is to give them the tools to convert this pain into their breakthrough power. I call this process Your Power Unleashed®.

My journey to unleashing my own power started with my personal struggle of trying to navigate the unfamiliar world of corporate America. I have hardworking immigrant parents—in particular, a mom who worked blue-collar jobs so that she could pay for my education. That opened the door for me to enter the corporate workforce. But when I got there, I had no frame of reference. Neither of my parents graduated from college. In fact, I now tearfully think of how proud I am that my mom and dad both decided to go back to school to get their GEDs as senior citizens. I pay homage to them for their grit, hard work, and undying optimism. They consistently told me to be grateful to be in this country, the United States of America, where I would have the opportunity to succeed. They knew that I might not have had this same privilege in the land of my birth, Jamaica. Yes, I'm grateful that they taught me the value of gratitude. But I had to be careful not to be too grateful to have a seat at the table that I'm unwilling to disrupt and shake up said table. Gratitude does not eradicate the need to advocate for, or expect, equity.

You see, for those of us who are immigrants, who are middle class, whose parents were blue-collar workers, or even those who are perhaps from single-parent households or from families of color—or insert your own specific story here—we're the women who weren't raised in homes where we were shown how to succeed in the corporate world. Although we worked hard to get the grades and the education that allowed us to be in these places, we've had to figure out how to move in these environments we're not familiar with, among people who don't look like us. And we have to do it all while looking like we know what the hell we're doing—confidently!

We don't often stop to analyze the absurdity of having to learn how to be confident and authoritative as a woman in a short period of time when, for most of our early lives as young girls, we've been taught to be humble, agreeable, and nice. Now, all of a sudden, as grown women in the workforce, we have to be powerful. What does that even mean? What does that look like?

This is why I wrote this book—to give women like us who were never expected to rise to the top in these spaces the insight needed to succeed here. This expertise I've gained through my own journey in the corporate space—from working alongside other savvy women who have effectively navigated these spaces, and from my experience successfully coaching women in various organizations over the past two decades. I will not only share advice and guidance with you but also practical strategies on how to skillfully tackle the system as your authentic self.

If your desire to live up to your full professional potential has been met with the pain of dealing with obstacles intent on holding you back, I am confident that the strategies in this book will help you reverse what may feel like a curse you're living in. You will step into your purpose and be that woman who courageously wins. When the world doesn't validate you, then you have to learn to validate yourself. This is what it means to unleash your power!

Your Power Unleashed® is a leadership development program I created and have now shared with hundreds of women of all ages who are at various points in their careers. It was birthed out of the need I saw for women to take back their power to determine what success looks like for them at work and in all areas of their lives. Over the last several years, it's been rewarding for me to see women break through their own self-doubt and limiting beliefs to cultivate the joy and inner peace that comes from being their authentic selves. This is not just liberating work; it's deeply healing.

I hope that as you read this book, you will undergo a transformation similar to that experienced by graduates of the Your Power Unleashed® program. I envision you fully owning and stepping into your greatness, feeling the profound relief that accompanies letting go of the constant pursuit of approval and validation. Instead, you will learn to provide these things for yourself, freeing yourself from reliance on others. Furthermore, I hope you will gain the confidence to play *bigger* in your life, leading to promotions, higher salaries, increased leadership opportunities, and the fulfillment of doing the work that you love. These external manifestations of success are the direct results of the courage and commitment required to look within and do deep, transformative personal development work.

Your Power Unleashed® is about recognizing the agency you have in determining the direction of your life and career, no matter what situation you're in. You get to choose when and how to use your power. In your choice lies your power. Let me say that again: your power lies in your ability to choose.

When we acknowledge and proactively use our power without waiting for anyone to give us permission to do so, we are, in fact, *owning* it. Many of us have seen the negative effects of power in our society, so the concept of "owning one's power" may be triggering. But this is not about using power in a toxic way over anyone else. Power is not good or bad. It's what we do with it that determines what it is. As women who will lead and transform every place that we set our feet on, we aspire to a different type of power than that inflicted by the patriarchy. We view power as something we embrace within ourselves. It is acknowledging the inner strength and confidence that have always been present inside of us. It's also about recognizing that this power is not a finite resource but rather a wellspring that grows stronger when *shared* with others—not used as a weapon to intimidate or manipulate them. We first seek to cultivate this power within ourselves so that we will live up to our full potential and be in positions of influence that will give us the authority to do more good in the world.

What You'll Find in This Book

The strategy in this book is intended to address both the internal and external barriers that prohibit us from living up to our full potential in the workplace.

This first part of the book, "Own Your Power," will help you master the inner game and lay the foundation for your success at work. Most books on career advancement give you tips and strategies on how to be effective at work, from interviewing for your dream role to being vocal about your desire for promotion, finding a mentor, and even negotiating your salary. The problem is that you can read hundreds of articles or books on the topic, but you will not consistently do the thing you intellectually know needs to be done if you haven't dealt with the limiting beliefs and sabotaging mindsets that get in the way of executing what you know.

So before we get to tactics, we will focus on mastering the inner game. As a trained leadership and executive coach, I will help you uncover ways of thinking that are unconsciously getting in the way of your success. We will work together to deprogram your mind from these patterns and create new ones that will serve you and the outcomes you desire. My purpose is to help you heal so that you can create a healthier relationship with your work identity and experience fulfillment in your vocation and in life.

Part II of Your Power Unleashed® focuses on smart workplace strategies that give you tactical tips on navigating the political landscape at work so that you can succeed there. Most of the women I've worked with over the years lament how they hate politics, but it's impossible to succeed in any organization—inside or outside of corporate—without understanding the unwritten rules at play that will determine your success. If you're not aware of these rules and how to steer through them, that naivete will become your glass ceiling. So make the decision not to be naive about how to navigate the corporate workplace but to be a savvy professional who takes charge of her career.

To close out the book, I embark on the first step in addressing the systems in which women work, starting with the executors of management systems: managers. Leadership in an organization has a unique ability to influence systems in the corporate space. Managers have a huge impact on whether or not the environment in which women work is one where they can thrive. This conclusion is therefore dedicated to equipping leaders—specifically men—who want to be more than just allies but sponsors and change agents dedicated to creating environments that will cultivate the success of the women in their teams through coaching. Coaching allows managers to not only partner with women in their professional development but also to transform the very culture of the workplace into one that allows everyone, regardless of background, to succeed.

Your Power Unleashed® is a courageous movement that invites everyone to stand for gender equality. People of all gender identities bring this message into their homes; to their daughters, sisters, mothers, and wives; into their communities; and into the broader organization in which they work. We choose not to advance alone, but together. An African proverb states: "If you want to go fast, go alone, but if you want to go far, go together."

Business Case Unleashed

Within each chapter, the Business Case Unleashed sidebar serves as a vital tool for leaders and decision-makers in organizations, bridging the gap between the personal and professional development topics discussed and tangible business outcomes. This section illustrates how the key subjects highlighted in a chapter transcend individual concerns to directly impact leadership effectiveness, decision-making processes, and overall company performance. By shedding light on the significance of addressing these crucial areas, the aim is to underscore their direct relevance in the workplace, while also providing the necessary motivation and clear business rationale for investing the company's time and resources in tackling these issues. Committing to addressing these topics as a company can yield a substantial return on investment, making it a strategic priority for organizational success.

BOLD Action

To facilitate the process of transformation, each chapter includes BOLD (Breaking Out of Limits Daringly) Actions. One of the mistakes I see people make is gathering a lot of information through reading and taking courses but not actually *experiencing* personal change because they have not implemented what they've learned. This section of the book converts what would otherwise be a textbook into a workbook, because both awareness and action have to be present for transformation to occur. Therefore, we'll commit to not being information junkies as we read this book but rather implementation masters. The BOLD Action steps as well as additional exercises in the chapters will help you do just that.

You will need a Your Power Unleashed® journal to complete the exercises, process emotional healing, write down insights or ideas, and keep track of your wins as a result of taking BOLD Actions. If you're someone who can't wait to get through the entire book, feel free to read it through quickly to get the general idea, but then go back and allow yourself to take the time to digest each chapter through reflection and action.

I suggest that you invite a friend to read this book with you or create a book club—aka a DIVA posse (DIVA is a term that I will define later in the book)—so that you can grow together with trusted friends, because the best transformation happens in community.

Intersectional Reflection Question

Being a woman affects how we encounter the world, but it doesn't shape the totality of our experiences in the workplace and in life. Intersectionality, a concept coined by scholar Kimberlé Crenshaw, recognizes that our experiences are multi-faceted, and shaped by various factors such as race, color, religion, sexual orientation, disability, culture, language, age, gender identity, immigration status, eye shape, indigenous identity, accent, hair texture, body size/shape, nationality, education, mental health status, class/socioeconomic status, and more. It is my aim to ensure that the work I do is inclusive of all our experiences. Traditional feminism failed to address the nuanced needs and experiences of diverse women, so in this book, I create space for you to contemplate your own unique journey.

While I intentionally feature stories of women of various backgrounds, I acknowledge that I cannot capture every possible nuance or perspective, but you can. You are invited to tell your own story and reflect on the totality of its impact, challenges, and victories. In the "BOLD Action" section, I have included an intersectional reflection question to create the space for this introspection. Intersectional reflection questions are powerful tools that expand our mindset to a more inclusive feminist approach, making room for nuance, learning, and broader perspectives. Your voice is powerful, your story is valuable, and your experiences matter. Embrace this opportunity to explore your truth, find healing, and experience transformation.

Unleashing the Next Chapter

At the end of each chapter, I share a short preview of what to expect in the upcoming one so that you can prepare yourself mentally to receive the transformation that's coming next and maintain your momentum all the way to the end of this book.

My Hope for You

We have enough external glass ceilings to smash through, so we don't need internal feelings of low self-worth to add to that list. There is an epidemic of women chronically underestimating themselves and abdicating their inherent power, but we can reverse this trend, one by one.

I wrote this book for the millions of women who want to take their power back and ensure that they are not inadvertently playing a role in their own oppression. I hope you will use the resources included here to self-heal, cultivate your talents and gifts, contribute at your highest level, create a legacy for your family and future generations of women, and live a life of purpose and contribution where you're recognized and abundantly rewarded for the value that you bring.

You may say, "Whoa, Kisha, this is just a career book, and that's a lot to put on one area of my life." Well, if you haven't figured it out by now, this book is much more than about your professional life. It's about who you're being and how you're showing up. When we change in one area, it affects every other area. In my own personal experience, since the workplace is where we earn a living and, therefore, an avenue for our financial survival, we're often more motivated to take action to improve in this area. If we can take this inherent motivation to change and use it as an integral part of our journey toward self-actualization, we can find joy, purpose, and meaning in the pursuit of our professional endeavors.

I invite you to also consider that we devote a substantial portion of our waking hours to our work. Therefore, if we find ourselves unfulfilled and merely going through the motions here, it means that a significant part of our existence is clouded by dissatisfaction. But it doesn't have to be this way.

My hope for you as you read this book is that you will envision a world where work will no longer be just a means to an end but rather a catalyst for personal growth and a platform to unleash your true potential. In this journey, I hope that you realize you're capable of so much more than you could ever imagine and have more power than you've been led to believe. As you engage with the material in this book, I pray that you will begin to unlock your magnificent potential and create environments around you that nurture and support your growth. As you do so, you will flourish, and all of your breakdowns will be converted into breakthroughs, which will allow you to have greater feelings of confidence, inspiration, and motivation that will create bigger and more rewarding opportunities for you professionally.

I hope that you will become an unstoppable force in your personal life, with everyone you come in contact with, and in shaping the culture in which you work. Although I can't promise that reading this book will fix the broken workplace systems that we operate in, my hope is that the leaders, executives, and decision-makers who read these words will experience their own personal transformations and use their personal journeys as a catalyst to ignite real change in corporate culture, starting with their own workplaces. We're all participants in this broken system and need to be better stewards of it. As each person owns and exercises the power that they have to make changes in their sphere of influence, I believe we will see a ripple effect from one person to another, one company to another, and one country to another.

Rev. Dr. Martin Luther King Jr. reminded us that "the arc of the moral universe is long, but it bends toward justice." Change takes a long time, but it does happen. If the people rise up to drive intentional change over time, the system will bend and must bend to us as we learn to unleash the magnificent power we all have within us.

My dear sisters, the time has come for you to rise up, own your power, and unleash it!

PART ONE

PART ONE

Own Your Power—
The Internal Work

PART ONE

PART ONE

PART ONE

CHAPTER ONE

UNDERSTANDING SELF-DOUBT (THE INNER CRITIC)

*No one can make you feel inferior without
your consent.*

—*Eleanor Roosevelt*

It was my first week in a new role as a global human resources leader of a Fortune 500 company's elite leadership development program. The organization took their most brilliant, high-potential employees from around the globe and put them on an accelerated trajectory to becoming the company's next vice presidents, presidents, CFOs, and CIOs. As I walked through the doors into the meeting room, where I knew almost no one, I thought, *Kisha, if you weren't in HR, you would never be in this room, because everyone who got accepted into this program is ten times smarter than you are. So put your poker face on, and just don't say anything that will expose you as being less than.*

The problem was that I *did* feel less than—I felt less smart than, less competent than, less qualified than, and many other types of "less." As a woman who has had to navigate corporate spaces where most people don't share my background and who may even doubt my abilities for whatever reason—whether it's because of my gender, race, national origin, skin color, accent, or even because of my youthful look (at the time!), I was used to putting on my armor. I might have been reeling inside with self-doubt and feeling not good enough, but one thing was for certain—I would never let them see me sweat!

Yes, that sounds very badass because, like many of you, I know how to put on the armor of badass as a matter of survival in corporate spaces. Brené Brown, in her book *Daring Greatly*,[1] talks about this concept of armor. According to her research, armor is a defense mechanism we use to protect ourselves from vulnerability and shame. When we're not operating in spaces that were designed for us to succeed in, places that don't always feel safe for us, putting on this protective covering becomes a matter of survival and allows us to feel less exposed.

The problem is that as our years at work turn into decades, this self-preserving shield begins to numb us from processing the difficult emotions that come with self-doubt. Although we may be able to project strength and confidence on the outside because we have to, the truth is that there is a lack of self-assurance within. High self-regard is an unwavering belief in ourselves, a feeling that we know beyond a shadow of a doubt that we have what it takes, regardless of our environment. We have become so detached from our internal world, however, that we no longer even recognize that we have internalized insecurities, and we are oblivious to their detrimental impact on our self-confidence and self-esteem.

Regardless of background, most of us are familiar with the voice in our head that plants seeds of doubt in our mind about our abilities. This is the voice that I'm referring to as self-doubt. It's that nagging, shaming, criticizing voice that shows up whenever we attempt to step outside of our comfort zone and try to play bigger. That voice showed up in my mind that day as I entered the meeting room. The crazy thing I learned as I spent months in that same organization and got to know the brilliant, high-potential leaders who participated in that meeting was that most of them had felt the way I did at some point during their careers. In fact, many continued to have those feelings on a regular basis. Later in this book, I will talk about just how common these feelings are, especially in competitive, high-performing environments; and how much more intense they are for people in organizations where the prototypes of successful top leaders don't look, sound like, or have similar personalities to them.

Many of us try to forcefully fight self-doubt because we understand just how insidious this voice is and how effective it can be in crushing our dreams before they even have a chance to blossom or grow. Self-doubt, sometimes called the inner critic, is a deadly poison that can kill our personal and professional potential if we don't stop it before it spreads like an aggressive form of cancer throughout our entire bodies.

The most effective way to stop self-doubt's deadly spread is not to overreact to it or to passively allow it to control our actions. Fighting and resisting this voice will only make it stronger, as illustrated by renowned Swiss psychiatrist Carl G. Jung's quote: "Whatever you resist persists." In these instances, self-doubt gets stronger because our energy is very focused on what that voice is saying, which results in it consuming us while growing bigger and bigger.

A more effective strategy for conquering self-doubt is to understand why it shows up, discern its purpose, and address the root cause rather than just reacting to the voice itself.

Why the Voice of Self-Doubt Shows Up

Growth and Transformation

The first reason why self-doubt shows up is because growth is happening. Growth takes place when we're doing something new or taking on a challenge that we've never taken on before. When you feel self-doubt, I invite you to pause and realize that this is, in fact, a reason to celebrate—because you, my friend, are not resting on your laurels trying to depend on someone else or the universe to make things happen for you. You're stepping up, taking action, and launching forward in your life. You're doing all these things even though they may be hard or challenging. This shows that you're being brave and in the process of a life-changing transformation.

Self-doubt is a sign of growth because it only shows up when you're stretching yourself outside of your comfort zone and playing big. It could be that you're preparing to present in front of a more senior-level audience than you've ever done in the past or that you're putting your name in the hat to apply for a more senior role. You're pushing against the tide. If you're not taking risks, if you're not living your dreams, if you're not stepping up to a new challenge, this voice will not show up. My first invitation to you, therefore, as you deal with the voice of self-doubt, is to be kind to yourself. Do not beat yourself up for feeling this manifestation of fear, especially in a workplace that's frequently not affirming to people who have your background.

Instead, I want you to celebrate yourself for the courage you've displayed in stepping up and taking action. Your action may be imperfect and messy, just as children learning to walk will fall down a few times until they find their footing—so is it when you're breaking through your comfort zone. The process will be messy until you take action in this area enough times to develop a deep level of competence. This new ability will become second nature to you, which will be evidence that it's encoded into your very nervous system. The goal isn't a one-time, inspired action, but an inner transformation of who you are and how you're showing up at the DNA level.

Self-doubt, my friend, is just an indication that life has presented you with an opportunity to grow and be transformed. So, let the transformation begin!

Your Brain Is Trying to Keep You Safe

Many of us assume that the primary purpose of our brain is to think rational thoughts, and therefore, we give way too much credit to the accuracy of the voice of self-doubt. But according to neuroscientist Lisa Feldman Barrett in the book *Seven and a Half Lessons about the Brain,*[2] the brain's primary purpose is to keep us alive and well. This means that the brain will construct processes to keep us safe, even if it needs to alter our interpretation of what is really happening to be successful in the pursuit of this goal.

This realization is liberating for two reasons. First, it helps you understand that the message from self-doubt that tells you that you're not good enough isn't an objective truth but rather is part of the brain's efforts to protect you from a perceived threat. The kicker is that the threat can be real or completely imagined. I will elaborate more on fear in chapter 4, but it's important to note that when our brain is operating from self-preservation, it will not be able to discern the difference between a real danger and one that's fabricated.

The second reason is that when you realize your brain is telling you a story to keep you safe (Barrett refers to these as *predictions*), then you can decide to *tell yourself a better story.* This more empowering narrative can inspire you to take action that leads to the results you desire, rather than keeping you trapped in fear. You can speak gently to your brain, saying something like,

"Brain, I know you're reacting and activating the fight, flight, or freeze response to try to keep me safe, but I'm strong enough to handle this situation. I got this!"

This is agency—the ability to act and exert power in your own life and over your own destiny rather than succumbing to a broken mindset tied to fear or to the oppressive system in which we do business. This understanding and empowering self-talk is the first step in breaking the shackles of fear that may have kept you bound for so long.

I provided some insight into the neuroscience of self-doubt to emphasize that this reaction is a common part of the human experience. My intention is that this information will help you move past the self-berating associated with an inner critic attack. It's my hope that, armed with this understanding, you can choose to embrace the strategies we will explore to effectively reduce any fear that will hinder you from living your best life.

Internalized Systemic Bias

Self-doubt will often show up in individuals who belong to marginalized groups and who feel the pressure to prove themselves in the face of societal biases. As women working in corporate spaces, we are in environments that weren't specifically designed for us. The business and professional world is, and has historically been dominated by men, built by them, and customized specifically for their needs. One clear example of this, highlighted in the book *The First, the Few, the Only*,[3] is the fact that Boeing engineers, who were mostly men in the 1970s, designed stowage that was accessible for the height of the average man. The average woman, however, has to compensate by tiptoeing and lifting a heavy bag over her head. The added fact that many women don't have a high level of upper body strength can cause them to feel unwelcome, not strong enough, and so on. Upon encountering these inconveniences on a plane, women may begin to worry that something is wrong with them rather than with the design of the aircraft (aka—the system). They internalize the bias in the system and blame themselves for something that's not their fault. Unfortunately, this blame frequently comes from external sources as well.

We women will go on to encounter biases, microaggressions, and discrediting in the professional and corporate worlds, which cause the unconscious adoption of societal attitudes and beliefs about ourselves, including toxic messages about our roles and what we can or cannot do. When women of color and women in general grow to believe these negative messages about their identity or just feel unseen and not considered, this leads to feelings of self-doubt and shame. We feel a lack of confidence—not because there is something inherently wrong with us, but because we're operating in a system that's laced with messages and practices that discredit us.

The system both deposits these insecurities and then evokes self-doubt in women by its very nature. Therefore, it's important to recognize and actively work to address these internalized biases by dismantling systemic practices that alienate us. We should strive to equip ourselves with the personal development tools needed to liberate ourselves from internalized oppression.

The Criticized Child: Early Wounding from Childhood

Childhood experiences, upbringing, and messages received during the formative years of your life can contribute to self-doubt. For example, if you struggled in school, were compared to other children who were seen as more successful, and were then criticized by an authority figure—whether it was a teacher, parent, or someone else—you might find yourself continuously trying to prove that you're enough during adulthood, even if the source of criticism is no longer in your life. This is because you experienced wounding of the inner child within you, which activated the inner critic.[4]

Authors Jay Earley and Bonnie Weiss, in their book *Freedom from Your Inner Critic*, discuss the concept of the *criticized child*. This refers to a part of us that represents the young inner child that internalized the inner critic's negative messages, leading us to feel worthless, defeated, and hopeless from a young age.[5] This can deeply affect the inner child, giving rise to an inner critic that uses shame as a tool. Some of the common ways the authors say wounding occurs at this impressionable time are when the inner child experiences the following:

- Judgment from key figures, leading to feelings of inadequacy or worthlessness

- Shame, frequently triggered by parents, teachers, peers, and others

- Judgments from family or society related to factors such as poverty, immigration status, or race

- Punitive control—overreactions to children's behavior by parents or others that can harm the child and activate a *harsh* inner critic

- Rejection or abuse leading to feeling unsafe or unworthy

- Diminishment, a response to a child being ridiculed for standing out, triggering an undermining critic that aims to keep the child small and unnoticed

Do you recognize childhood experiences related to any of the above that fueled feelings of self-doubt in you? These early wounds from childhood can hold you back from living life to the fullest. In fact, experiences like this sometimes lead to children developing lifelong habits of being harsh to themselves instead of being kind. However, as we acknowledge these incidents, we can guide ourselves to heal and re-parent our inner critic, ultimately fostering a healthier self-perception and emotional well-being.

Deconstructing Self-doubt Statements Holding You Back

Self-doubt, aka the inner critic, usually says the same thing to us repeatedly to get us to shrink back from taking action, and it normally includes some form of not being enough. Here are some inner critic statements I've compiled from the women I've coached over the years.

- I'm not good enough.
- I'm not smart enough.
- My accent is too thick.
- I'm too much.
- I'm not enough.
- I'm too young.
- I'm too old.
- I have no value to add.
- I don't have enough experience.
- I'm overqualified.
- What if I'm wrong?
- Everyone will find out that I'm a fake.

Do any of these sound familiar to you? Are there other statements that recur in your mind that slow you down or cause you to play smaller in some way? If so, The following exercise inspired by Lisa Nichols' work will help you diminish the impact of these insidious lies.

Personal Transformation Activity:

New Pillars Exercise

Step 1: Get a sheet of paper and fold it in two halves vertically. On the left side, write down three to five statements you most frequently hear from your internal critic. You could consider these your *core* self-doubts or the old pillars upon which many of your other doubts are built because they occur repeatedly in your brain. These recurring messages are ones that you've bought into or believed and have become second nature. These statements are normally, but not always, related to some version of not being good enough, not belonging, or some other negative thing. Leave five lines between each statement, and write each one with a color that's boring/dull; a pencil is a great option. Title this left column *Self-Limiting Pillars*.

Did you do it yet? If not, stop reading now, as proceeding further will lessen the impact of this exercise. It only takes three minutes, and when you do it, you will enjoy a transformation you didn't expect. *Do not* read ahead. Stop now and do the activity. Your transformation does not lie in merely reading this book—but when you *apply* the knowledge.

Step 2: On the other (right) side of the folded page, I want you to write with your favorite bright-colored pen in the column titled *Inspirational Pillars*. The left column contains limiting thoughts that constrain you, but the right column is meant to inspire you and open you up to possibilities. These will be new pillars upon which you will build a strong foundation for your confidence.

Step 3: Parallel to each left column, *Self-Limiting Pillars* statement, I want you to write a new series of four sentences that represent inspirational possibilities for the limiting thought and put those in the *Inspirational Pillars* column. Don't try to write anything really extravagant that you can't accept or believe but rather write simple, positive statements that reflect new possibilities that inspire and stretch you a bit. Pause, listen to what your heart is telling you, and then capture it by writing it down. If you feel that the new possibility is too much of a stretch for you to believe about yourself right now, start the sentence with "There is a part of me that knows . . ." and end with ". . . I open up myself to experience this possibility as a reality in my life now."

Here is my example from a few years ago:

My original core self-doubt sentence: I'm not smart enough.

Four inspirational possibilities I chose to believe instead of this self-limiting statement were:

1. I'm a brilliant writer and coach. I open up myself to experiencing more and more of this possibility as a reality in my life now.

2. I know that I'm a smart woman because I've provided innovative solutions that have substantially benefited my clients and organizations.

3. There's a part of me that knows that I'm absolutely brilliant because I've had many conversations with other brilliant people who have found my contributions helpful and insightful. I open up myself to experiencing more of this as a reality in my life now.

4. There is a part of me that knows that whatever I don't know now, I'm resourceful enough to figure it out, just as I've done in the past. I open myself up to experiencing this possibility as a reality in my life now.

Notice that, in the first two sentences, I did not open up with "There's a part of me that knows" because, at the time, I was (and still am) very confident in my intelligence as well as my writing and coaching skills, so I didn't have to include that qualifier. If you have a high level of confidence regarding any of the affirmations that you write, you can also leave off both the preface and the closing of the affirmation. Note that I did not say anything like "I'm smarter than all my co-workers and everyone I meet." My subconscious mind would never accept this as a reality because I know it's not true, and it also violates my value of not being overly competitive with others or comparing myself to them.

It's important to use positive statements, because the subconscious mind rejects statements made in the negative, such as "I'm not dumb," and will be more receptive to an affirmative statement, such as "I am brilliant." Lisa Nichols, in her book *Abundance Now*,[6] explains how important it is to write affirmations for effectiveness, based on what you want to create rather than on what you want to avoid.

Step 4: Read these positive statements out loud daily, preferably at night before you go to bed, as the subconscious mind becomes more active and receptive right before you go to sleep. You can also do so in the morning or any other time of the day to keep reprogramming your mind. Repeat this for twenty-one days to begin the process of creating new mental habits that will fuel you.

There was a member of my Your Power Unleashed coaching program who experienced inner critic statements regarding her accent as a Cuban woman living in the US.

Her original core self-limiting sentence was: My accent makes me anxious about my communication skills and makes me doubt my effectiveness.

Her new inspirational statements were:

1. There's a part of me that knows that my accent makes me unique and differentiates me. I open up myself to experiencing this possibility as a reality in my life now.

2. There is a part of me that knows that many people love my accent and think it's beautiful [which she knew was true after a few of the women in our program told her so]. I open up myself to experiencing this possibility as a reality in my life now.

3. There is a part of me that knows my accent reflects my rich cultural heritage and history. I open up myself to experiencing this truth as a reality in my life now.

Another program member from New York City experienced inner criticism based on her mother telling her she was lazy, so she found it hard to rest or relax. This person found herself at a high level of burnout when she came into my program. Her burnout was the result of trying too hard to prove unconsciously to her now deceased mother that she was good enough because she worked hard. Unfortunately, the downside to this work was that it was detrimental to her health.

Her original core self-limiting sentence was: I have to prove my worth through my achievements, no matter what the cost.

Her inspirational affirmations were:

1. There is a part of me that knows that I need to rest so that I can be restored. I choose to operate in this reality in my life now.

2. There is a part of me that knows I'm enough, so I don't need to prove my worthiness through unhealthy workloads. I choose to operate in this reality in my life now.

3. There is a part of me that desires the gift and the grace to enjoy life. I choose to operate in this reality in my life now.

4. I give myself permission to lovingly care for and be kind to myself.

5. I release the lie that overworking is a source of honor for me.

As you complete this exercise, I know that it will become clear to you that the inner critic is not a truth speaker but instead uses lies, in a misguided way, to try to protect you from harm. These affirmations that you create will be part of your strategy to dismantle the lies of the inner critic.

Business Case Unleashed

Why companies need to address employees' self-doubts (productivity and cost savings).

In our work with organizations, we have found that self-doubt among employees has a detrimental impact on organizational productivity. When employees spend their time questioning their decisions and abilities, it leads to delayed action, analysis paralysis, and ultimately, missed opportunities. However, when they overcome this mental pattern, it leads to higher-quality output, increased efficiency, and greater proactivity. This transformation not only enhances overall productivity but also unlocks substantial cost savings for the company.

Common Inner Critic Strategies

The inner critic has some very common ways to operate, so in order for you to identify when it's in operation, here are a few of its strategies.

Unkind Judger: The inner critic berates you, criticizes you, blames you, and shames you. It speaks to you in an unkind way that you would never use to speak to a loved one or a friend.

Comparison: It compares you to others and makes you feel as if you're always behind. It amplifies the achievements of others while simultaneously undervaluing and diminishing yours.

Self-Blame: It attributes failures to personal deficits without looking holistically at the situation, taking into consideration external factors (including systemic bias) and circumstances that could have contributed to the outcome. This also hinders your ability to find the root cause of why you may have failed and to think of ways you can avoid these mistakes in the future.

Overgeneralization: This is when you take one negative experience or mistake and apply it to every area of your life. This leads you to underestimate and incorrectly assess your abilities.

Catastrophizing: This causes you to overreact to things and blow them out of proportion without being able to test the reality of your thinking. It imagines the worst-case scenarios, which in actuality are unlikely to occur. The result is that it stops you from challenging distorted thinking patterns so that you can make more accurate assessments about what's going on.

"Should" Statements: You set rigid rules for yourself using phrases such as *should, must,* or *have to.* This triggers feelings of shame and inadequacy when you fall short.

Based on Predictions: As we learned in the concept of the criticized child, the inner critic is fueled by past experiences. Even though we're in the present moment, our brain begins to interpret what is happening based on past events rather than allowing us to test the reality of whether this experience is truly the same as what happened before (often from childhood). This imperceptible brain process is described well by Lisa Feldman Barrett in her book *How Emotions Are Made: The Secret Life of the Brain.*[7]

She explains this process as the theory of constructed emotion, which states that "in every waking moment, your brain uses past experience, organized as concepts, to guide your actions and to give your sensations meaning." Our brain gives meaning to a sensation that we're experiencing in our body, and these meanings, which Barrett calls *predictions*, are based on past experiences that will instruct your body on how to cope or react. The issue is that predictions are not always correct. We make prediction errors based on the past, which is not aligned with the reality that's currently in front of us. What we need to do is utilize practical methods that will slow down this rapid prediction process so that we can accurately assess what is going on and then choose an empowering response.

Creates Sexy Excuses That Delay Action: These excuses always require more preparation—especially in the form of training or speaking to someone else, but you never get to the point of being ready. The truth is, yes, sometimes you do need more training. But more often than not, what you need to do is to act now! When I feel the urge to delay action, I tell myself, "Kisha, you are a *now* person." Will you also decide to be a *now* person rather than use a highly deceptive excuse that delays action? Repeat after me, "I'm a *now* person!"

People-Pleasing: As humans, we have a desire for connection and belonging, so we will try to make others happy to gain acceptance. But the problem is that we frequently do so at the expense of our own needs and convictions. When we haven't developed a practice of validating ourselves, we'll seek validation from others. The truth is, when we like ourselves first by living in alignment with our own values, other people liking us will be the icing on the cake versus the entire cake itself!

Three Types of Inner Critics That Hijack Professional Women's Effectiveness

In addition to the strategies or tactics of the inner critic, there are specific types of inner critics that consistently usurp the impact of professional women and impede their ability to operate at their full potential. These manifestations of the inner critic can show up at different times in the same individual or concurrently to bring progress to a full stop. As you read each manifestation, I invite you to assess if you've experienced any one of them—or, as many of my clients confirm, all three—impacting your effectiveness at work.

1. The Imposter Treatment, not Syndrome—"I'm not a fraud."

The term *impostor syndrome* was coined in 1978 by two American clinical psychologists, Pauline Clance and Suzanne Imes. They determined based on a study[8] they conducted that impostor syndrome is a feeling of intellectual phoniness in people who believe that they are not capable despite their outstanding accomplishments. While these people are very achievement oriented, they also live in fear of being "found out" or exposed as frauds.

Clance and Imes's study revealed that impostor syndrome was particularly prevalent and intense among a select sample of high-achieving women. According to the study, in early family dynamics and later in life, the internalization of sex-role stereotyping, aka bias, appeared to contribute significantly to the development of the impostor feeling.

In recent times, famous women such as Maya Angelou, Sheryl Sandberg, Supreme Court Justice Sonia Sotomayor, and even former first lady Michelle Obama have all admitted to experiencing this phenomenon. It's important, however, to explore and address how systemic biases and noninclusive structures in the workplace exacerbate this impostor feeling in women. In fact, author and social justice warrior Elizabeth Leiba in her book *I'm Not Yelling: A Black Woman's Guide to Navigating the Workplace,*[9] thoroughly explores the premise that the issue women experience is not so much about having impostor syndrome as being treated like impostors. It's not an internal personality flaw, as we've been led to believe, that makes women feel inferior; rather it's the way we're treated in male-dominated spaces that leads us to internalize our experiences.

Regardless of where these feelings originate, in the spirit of agency over our own destinies, I take the stance that we still need to figure out how to address this feeling internally within ourselves while we work to dismantle the inequities in our systems. We have been waiting a long time for equity, but the truth is, no one is coming to save us. According to the 2023 World Economic Forum report,[10] it will take 131 years to close the overall gender gap. The system must be fixed, yes, but for those of us who are too impatient to wait 131 freaking years for that to happen, we need to work on getting our own mindset right and healing from the internal effects of systemic bias by addressing fear, impostor treatment, and self-doubt in all their forms.

2. The Indecisive Expert—"My only value is my knowledge."

Indecisive experts rely too much on their expertise to prove their worthiness and value. As a result, they overanalyze options and are ultimately afraid of making the wrong choices. In a society that places a high regard on professional expertise, we may not realize that a disordered relationship with expertise can be a symptom of self-doubt. This person wants to get every piece of information before they can decide or take action in an area. They use their expertise with a perfectionist mindset, which slows down their ability to engage in forward movement. They have an unquenchable thirst for information that causes them to focus on training and other preparation mechanisms rather than executing their goals. I refer to them as *information junkies* because they get their fix of knowledge like a shot in the arm and then enter this place of hallucination, deceiving themselves into thinking that they have done something. But they allow fear or rumination to stop them from applying this knowledge.

All the degrees, experiences, qualifications, accolades, courses, books, and training that they have invested in have not propelled them to step up and just do the darn thing. Information hoarding is just another way to procrastinate or to avoid doing the hard and scary thing, which is facing the fear of rejection and of not being enough. If you're one of the millions of women who don't apply for a job or raise your hand for a project unless you meet 100 percent of the qualifications, the indecisive expert may be at play in your life.

We must realize that there is a level of expertise that will never be attained until we take action. There are things that we will never learn just from reading a book, but only the challenge of embracing the uncertainty and discomfort that we have to work through in real-life applications will mature our book learning into practical and usable expertise.

3. The Perfectionist—"I have to be flawless."

Another inner critic manifestation is the perfectionist, which I refer to as the *perfectionist deception*. It's deceptive because, while being a perfectionist sounds like a noble goal, perfectionism isn't motivated by excellence. In fact, it comes from a place of self-doubt, that we're not good enough, so we have to prove our worth by never making a mistake. When we don't trust ourselves or see the value that we bring, we move from a strong work ethic and diligence to fanatic perfectionism, which depletes our energy and resourcefulness. This becomes counterproductive to producing outstanding results. Additionally, perfectionism keeps us too busy being the worker bee rather than being a strategic thought leader who's seen as someone capable and ready to lead rather than someone who is just carrying out everyone else's vision. Find out if you have perfectionist habits that are killing your career by taking the quiz below and giving yourself one point for every question that you answer yes to.

Quiz: Am I a Perfectionist?

Question	Yes/No
Do you set very high and unrealistic goals for yourself (almost unattainable) and then beat yourself up for not attaining them?	
Do you prefer to do the work yourself because you're the only one who can do it right (problem delegating)?	
Do you analyze, plan, and focus on improving your work but never actually launch (analysis paralysis)?	
Do you talk/think about your dreams and goals but usually delay taking action?	
Do you focus on the busywork rather than the strategic work that will get you recognition and results? (You may also think, I'm not sure what's strategic versus busywork.)	
Are you always trying to get ready but never feel quite ready?	
Do you think about what needs to get done but rarely take the time to celebrate the wins?	
Do you feel anxiety and stress from all the work that needs to be done, and it only seems to pile on?	

When you make a mistake, do you have a hard time letting go—which leads to feelings of being a failure or not being good enough?	
When you don't feel totally confident in your work, do you usually procrastinate from taking action?	

Interpretation of Results

If your score was:

- 0–3: Congratulations! Perfectionism doesn't slow you down or sabotage you from taking action.

- 4–6: Perfectionism affects you sometimes, but you normally figure out a way to get out of paralysis and into action. The trick for you will be minimizing delays that happen as you work through the mindset shifts needed. The strategies in this and the upcoming chapters will help you speed up the process.

- 7+: Perfectionism is playing a significant role in holding you back from achieving your highest potential in business and other areas of your life. But don't worry. The contents of this book will set you well on your way to defeating this sabotage mechanism in your life.

Let's Get Real about Perfectionism

The implications of perfectionism are profound, far-reaching, and even detrimental to personal and professional growth. In women, perfectionist behavior makes us overly cautious and hesitant to make daring moves in business and in life until we're certain of achieving success. This is the problem with perfectionism; it causes people to set excessively high standards and unrealistic expectations that are extremely difficult to attain, which holds them in a prison of paralysis due to a desire to do everything perfectly without error. The effects of perfectionism include critical self-evaluation and an obsessive level of fear about what others will think. This hinders us from stepping up to take on new challenges and delays the very action that could be the seed for our breakthrough.

Excellence versus Perfection

There is nothing wrong with having high standards—this is a noble goal when working toward excellence. As you may know, in the corporate world, there is no quicker way to destroy one's credibility than not knowing your stuff down cold. Therefore, preparing thoroughly is extremely important to being an effective professional. This is excellence, which is a process focused on consistent improvement and growth. However, having unrealistic expectations is perfectionism, and it sets you up for failure since it's completely unattainable. Perfectionism is like an elusive destination—the location keeps changing, so you never actually arrive.

According to blogger Marc Winn,[11] perfectionism is focused on "doing the thing *right*," which is centered on how things appear and if others think it's done correctly. Excellence is, however, about doing the right thing. Excellence is strategic and goes beyond surface-level superficial thinking—it's focused on the reason for a task and the *results* required for the endeavor to be a success.

Perfectionism steals time, drains energy, causes self-criticism, and gives rise to the inner critic. You begin to think that whatever you do is never good enough and that you, as a person, are not enough. Your identity and the quality of your work become completely intertwined. In contrast, excellence focuses on what matters and fills you with energy, creativity, and solution-oriented possibilities.

According to author Ralph Marston, excellence is not a skill but an attitude. This attitude of excellence stems from the core of your identity, which has been established by repeated actions.

Aristotle rightly described the process of excellence in his quote: "We are what we repeatedly do. Excellence then is not an act but a habit." If you develop the attitude of excellence, you will not be driven by the fear and anxiety of perfectionism—rather you will be pulled by a vision greater than yourself.

How to Disentangle from Perfectionism

Start with Realistic Expectations That Stretch You but Don't Crush You

If you aim for perfection in everything, you will achieve nothing. When you set excessively high-performance standards and focus on trying to attain the unattainable, this results in being overwhelmed and leads to despair, which wastes time as well as physical, mental, and emotional energy. This lost energy could have been focused on doing the innovative and transformational work that will get you recognized as a thought leader. Although it's critical to develop skills, build expertise, and practice effective techniques, there comes a time when you just have to go for it!

Move Forward While Silencing the Inner Critic

Perfectionists are overly critical with their self-evaluations and concerns regarding what other people think. When we listen to the critical voices in our heads, we risk silencing and crushing our unique, resourceful voices, our perspectives that bring immense value, and our differentiated talent that makes us indispensable. The voice of the inner critic prevents us from unleashing this inner genius, and it's essential to manage it in order to crush perfectionism.

Finish Your Work without Overidentifying with It

When we overidentify with our work, we run the risk of believing that our worth and value are based on how well we produce or on how others assess the quality of our work. When things are going well, perfectionists feel like they are valuable and important, but if things do not go perfectly, then their self-esteem goes down the drain. Breaking out of this soul-crushing cycle starts by believing that, as much as you want your work to be accepted, you're still valuable, no matter what the response is. Understand the truth—that if people love your work, you are worthy of love, admiration, and respect; and if they don't love your work, you are still worthy. Their response is not an indictment of who you are as an individual—it's merely emotionally neutral data on whether or not the work met their expectations.

We need to learn to take people's impressions of our work as information on what we will decide to do or not do to meet their expectations. Hopefully, as we all practice excellence and bravery rather than perfectionism, we will learn how to break out of our self-imposed limitations and feel more confident in sharing our unique ideas unapologetically. I hope you will be less afraid of criticism, knowing that other people's opinions of you do not define who you are, and they only have the power over you that you give them.

Finally, I hope that as you're liberated from trying to prove your worth through your work, you will begin to prioritize taking care of yourself by resting more and engaging in therapeutic activities that will help restore you so that you can avoid working to the point of burnout.

Remember, you're not only good enough, but you're a brilliant light, so let your brilliance shine bright just like a diamond does.

***

Unleashing the Next Chapter

If you have ever wanted to learn how to transform the demotivating inner critic into an energizing inner coach that will revolutionize the way you tackle challenges, overcome obstacles, and elevate how you see yourself, let's proceed to chapter 2 after you do the BOLD Actions below!

BOLD Actions to Evoke Your Transformation

1. Have you ever been in a situation that stretched you so far outside of your comfort zone that you began to doubt your ability to navigate it? Describe the situation and what you learned about yourself from this experience.

2. Which one of the reasons given that self-doubt shows up resonated the most with you and caused a shift in your perspective?

   a. Growth and transformation

   b. Your brain trying to keep you safe

   c. Internalized systemic bias

   d. The criticized child

3. Which type of experience did you have in childhood that activated a wounding of the criticized child (judgment, shame, punitive control, rejection, abuse, or diminishment)?

4. ***Intersectional reflection question:*** *Are there any parts of your identity (e.g. age, weight, immigration status, etc.) that you have internalized negative messages and biases from society? How has this influenced your self-confidence and how you feel about yourself?*

5. What insights or breakthroughs did you get from the New Pillars exercise? Have you put a reminder on your calendar for the next twenty-one days to remind you

to say your newly created affirmations out loud before going to bed?

6. Of the common inner critic strategies, which one occurs most frequently for you?

7. How will understanding the difference between excellence and perfectionism transform how you approach your work and tasks?

8. Take the Am I a Perfectionist? quiz.

CHAPTER TWO

FROM INNER CRITIC TO INNER COACH TO INNER DIVA

If there is no enemy within, the enemy outside can do us no harm.

—African proverb

I sat in front of the chief executive officer as part of the final rounds of interviews in this organization. It was my first time having a one-on-one conversation of any kind with an officer of a Fortune 20 company who was not in the human resources area. I get HR people, and they get me, so that was my comfort zone. But CEOs? This was new. I knew, intellectually, that this man was just a normal human being, but somehow my body—specifically my heart and palms—didn't register this fact.

This interview felt high-stakes. This was the man sitting between me and the biggest career jump I'd ever had in my life. Not only was this a huge potential promotion, but I could not remember ever being so excited about doing a role outside of my first job after graduating from college. This was the problem; I wanted the job too much, and in front of this CEO with the biggest presence, I felt like a fraud. The worst part was that his penetrating gaze felt so intruding that I swear he could literally see and hear the thoughts screaming in my head that said, "You were able to fool the HR folks, but you won't be able to fool him into thinking you're ready for this job. You don't have the experience. You're a fraud, and he's going to see it." I was so preoccupied with this internal dialogue that I didn't realize he'd asked me a question. As I came back to the room from the voyage in my mind, I heard him say, "Tell me about yourself."

I'd practiced answering this question all week, so this should have been easy-breezy. I knew what to say, but as I opened my mouth, I could not speak. I knew enough about the fight-or-flight response to know that I was officially in this state. The salivary production had officially stopped, causing my mouth to be so parched that it was difficult to articulate even a single word. I was in survival mode.

As if that wasn't enough, I had a sudden muscle contraction in my right hamstring at that exact moment, and the pain was so sharp that I bit my lower lip forcefully in an attempt to stifle the overwhelming rush of emotions that threatened to trigger tears to fall down my cheeks as they welled up in my eyes. *Kisha, you'd better not cry. Don't cry. Do not cry.*

As I scolded myself into showing a tough exterior, the CEO realized something was going on, and this benevolent person gently asked, "Are you okay? Do you need a glass of water?"

I could only manage to give a slight nod, and he got up and grabbed a bottle of ice-cold water from the mini fridge in his extravagant office, which gave off an air of grandeur. This setting did not help. He placed the water on the mahogany desk in front of me. Somehow, as I sipped the water, I told myself what a privilege it was to be sitting here, and no matter what the outcome of this interview, this was an experience I could learn and grow from. This new internal dialogue calmed me down, and I recovered enough to answer his questions. He was a firm, stern, yet kind man. His presence took up the entire office, and as I leaned into the conversation, I realized this was part of what had initially intimidated me. I was, however, resilient in the moment and got through it.

Fast-forward to the end of the week. I got the job offer, winning out over several others who had also interviewed, including people who worked internally in that organization. That experience, however, was the catalyst for discovering the inner critic, specifically the impostor syndrome. Getting the job was great, but I knew that if I was to attain any other level of career success beyond that point, I needed to learn how to effectively tame the inner critic when it raised its ugly head. I therefore embarked on a journey of research, training, and coaching to understand this phenomenon.

The tactics in this chapter result from years of research, training, and practice I've used on myself and the hundreds of women and men I've coached over the last fifteen-plus years. As we continue our conversation about the different ways to tame the inner critic, I recommend that you lean into the principles below as you determine a strategy to conquer this situation in your own life.

Four Principles to Embrace Before You Attempt to Tame the Inner Critic

1. Normalize and Destigmatize

One of the best ways to limit the impact of the inner critic is to shine a light on the truth, which is that it's very common to the human experience. Since most people have had some experience with the inner critic, it's helpful to name and normalize the phenomenon as the first step to taming its effects. It blows my mind whenever I deliver keynote speeches on this topic that there are so many people of all backgrounds raising their hands to confirm that they, too, have had an encounter with it. This is why the neuroscience around this is so helpful to many, and why I address it early in this book. When we realize that we're not weird, strange people who are uniquely flawed but rather that experiencing self-doubt is part of the universal human experience, this realization removes the impact of shame and the debilitation that comes with it. We can then move on to useful strategies in order to neutralize its effect.

In the coaching programs I've led throughout the years, this is one of the biggest benefits that participants say they experience, realizing that so many have heard these messages. You can tap into the power of a supportive community by talking to a few trusted friends and asking them if there was ever a time when they thought that they didn't belong or weren't good enough. This inquiry will further prove to you just how common self-doubt is, even with the people you know, including men. You will also be astounded to realize how similar the messages are.

2. Name and Tame

Naming the inner critic for what it is can help you reduce its impact, because you know it's not really your authentic self talking. This mental process is just an age-old defensive mechanism triggered by the fight-or-flight response because growth is happening, and you're attempting to step up your game. Whenever you experience debilitating self-doubt, you can overcome it by calling it what it is—an irrational fear or a natural protective mechanism. You can then work on calming down by taking a few deep breaths and adopting one of the taming strategies that we will discuss so that you can reengage the logical regions of your brain, including the prefrontal cortex, and decide how you want to respond to the situation at hand rather than just subconsciously reacting to it in a way that doesn't serve you. In the end, you will realize that the majority of the time, you're not and never were in life-threatening danger.

3. Just Try One Strategy at a Time

I will provide a variety of strategies to choose from in the upcoming section, but it's not necessary and, in fact, is counterproductive to try all of them at once. This is because some strategies may resonate with you and some won't, so you will need to experiment one at a time to see which ones help you. I recommend that you pick one strategy that seems to resonate with you, experiment with it for a few weeks, and if it works, awesome, that's your strategy. If it doesn't work for you, try another one for a few weeks, and keep going through the process until you identify your preference.

4. The Inner Critic Is Not the Real You, but Rather the Wounded, Criticized Child

In chapter 1, we reviewed the concept of the criticized child that activated the inner critic as a result of wounding experiences. If you therefore find yourself reacting in a disempowering way to a situation because of the inner critic, instead of tying your identity to the reaction itself, separate from it by observing and witnessing what is happening. This process of observing and witnessing is referred to as awareness in various mindfulness practices. We can simply be aware of our reactions and emotions without becoming them.

For example, instead of saying, "I'm nervous," which subconsciously makes you take on the identity of being a nervous person, get curious and think about the experience from the perspective of an observer. This shift in perception separates you from identifying as the experience of nervousness you're facing without suppressing this feeling or denying it. In this scenario, we embrace the curiosity that comes from observing and say to ourselves, "Nervousness is happening. I wonder what the root cause is." This intentional pondering leads to discovery and is the prerequisite for creating a strategy to address the situation.

A Word on Identity

This concept of forming an identity around our learned stress response is such an important one because, over time, we learn to create false personas around defense mechanisms that we develop as a reaction to pressure and trauma. Stressful situations can cause us to worry, for example, which is a natural and adaptive reaction in many scenarios. Where we err is when we label ourselves as worriers, which is a fake identity that we take on that leads to more consistent behaviors in line with this created character—but ultimately does not serve us. In chapter 5, I talk about how to use courage to shed fake identities and step into who we authentically are. In the meantime, we can open ourselves up to the possibility that we are warriors, not worriers!

Transform Your Inner Critic into Your Inner Coach

A coach is different from the inner critic in that she speaks to herself with compassion and curiosity while striving for accountability in taking actions that will evoke transformation. In this section, we will focus on adopting the mindset of a coach with specific skill sets that will help you transform the inner critic into the inner coach.

A coach is someone who provides support and guidance to facilitate growth and achievement. As coaches, we hold our inner beings tenderly in a container of respect, esteem, and belief that we're capable, creative, and resourceful. If we come from this empowering place when working through a self-doubt trigger, we will not ask ourselves disempowering and critical questions like "Why are you so stupid?" Instead, we will ask curious, value-generating questions like "What has caused me to act in a way that's not in line with what I truly desire and in line with whom I aspire to be?" Asking yourself a powerful question like this can help you fully uncover the underlying blockage to your stepping up, whether that underlying cause is rooted in fear or trauma from a past experience.

Powerful questions are essential tools in coaching yourself and others because they help you gain a deeper understanding of yourself, encourage self-reflection that can lead to personal transformation, and pull the magic of creativity and problem-solving out of your soul. The coaching chapter in this book is dedicated to equipping male leaders in organizations to use coaching as a tool to accelerate growth in their female employees and to drive inclusivity in their organizational culture. However, in this chapter, I am focusing on women learning how to coach themselves, because the best person to first practice your coaching skills on is yourself.

Below are some examples of the different mindsets a coach has toward us versus how the inner critic sees us.

Inner Critic	Inner Coach
Sees you as a fragile child, in need of protecting and being kept safe.	Sees you as capable of dealing with the challenges you face by tapping into your inner power, which gives you agency.
Sees you as a novice needing to be told what to do.	Regards you as resourceful; whatever you don't know right now, you can figure out.
Thinks that if you fall (make a mistake), you will stay down.	Knows you're resilient so even if you fall 777 times, you will rise back up again.

Has a fixed mindset, focused on avoiding failure.	Has a growth mindset, willing to step up to take risks, knowing that failure is actually a vehicle to learn and grow.
Makes you feel as if you're not enough.	Helps you see that all you need is already within you and gives you tools to bring out your best self.

Activate the Inner Coach: Seven Resources You Can Use to Coach Yourself

1. Reframing

Reframing is a cognitive tool that allows you to apply a perspective to your experiences, which gives you back your power. It's a technique that helps you build the skill of resiliency and is extremely useful in taming the voice of self-doubt. When you reframe an event that has occurred in your life, the facts will remain the same, but a deliberate mental shift is made in how you interpret it.

In the interview story that I shared to open this chapter, I didn't know it at the time, but I reframed the interview experience that I was having in the moment to tell myself what a privilege I had to even have the opportunity to interview. I repositioned my outlook as the following: no matter what the outcome is, it will be a great learning experience. This reframing calmed me down by allowing me to see that because I had gotten this far in the interview, I had already won, no matter what happened next.

I've since gone on to embrace a very helpful perspective that I've heard from friends, which says, "There is no such thing as failure; either I win, or I learn." I had allowed the stakes regarding the outcome of this interview to be so high that I panicked and activated the physiological fight-or-flight response. When I reframed it as a learning experience, it reduced the stakes and allowed me to reengage in the interview in a calm state.

I've also learned that instead of looking at the inner critic as a powerful enemy, like a monster we have to defeat, we can reframe it so that it doesn't seem like such a big and overwhelming obstacle. We can view the inner critic as a compassionate yet clueless friend who is trying to help us in the best way she knows how. Her ways of handling the challenge we're facing, though well intentioned, are toxic, and by knowing this, we can then calmly respond to her efforts.

One conversation that my clients have found helpful to have with the internal critic is to say, "Dear one, I know that you're trying to protect me from being rejected or experiencing failure, but I got this. I'm strong, and I can handle this situation, whatever happens. Even if the worst thing happens (though it rarely does), I'm resilient and will bounce back."

Do you feel the energetic shift in this statement? When you're fighting a perceived beast, it may feel insurmountable. And the more you fight against it, the stronger it seems to get. Yet the gentle, less-draining reframing above allows you to release yourself from the clutches of fear with a better sense of control and centeredness.

2. Connect to Your Higher Values

One of the most powerful antidotes to the inner critic is connecting to your values. Values are a judgment of what's important in your life, and if you connect to a powerful enough value that you have, it can stop the inner critic in its tracks. How I handled the aforementioned interview with the CEO included an aspect of connecting to my values. Learning and growth are big values for me, so when I reframed the experience to connect to learning, it helped me feel fulfilled. If I got at least one lesson from this experience, that alone would make it worthwhile, whether or not I was offered the role. I knew the lessons would help me attain the next big opportunity, even if I didn't get that one.

If self-doubt has paralyzed you from playing as big in the world as you desire, connecting to your core values can help you tap into a source of motivation and internal drive that will allow you to move past fear's blockage. If you're unsure what your driving values are, rest assured that the ones discussed in chapter 3 will give you the clarity you need. Your values will provide fortitude to push through fear so that the inner critic will absolutely not have the final word, but your inner coach and your higher purpose will.

I invite you to ask yourself, "What's more important to me than my fears?" Make this thing your motivation for stepping up to play big today.

3. Bring in Your Love Advocate

The inner critic is the harsh judge who violently wields shame and condemnation against you. It speaks to you in a toxic way. No one would intentionally speak like this to someone they love. So bring an advocate of love into situations where the inner critic begins to accuse you. When the enemy of fear rears its ugly head, we need the love advocate to fight for the wholeness of our hearts.

Imagine you are defending your loved one who is struggling in the same areas as you are, but you are much kinder and more loving to them; in other words, you aren't judgmental. Write down the accusations and negative statements the inner critic has made about you. Now, with the kindness, love, and compassion you have in your heart for your dearest friend, speak on their behalf, come to their rescue, and be their hero. This is the language that you will read back in support of yourself.

Your love advocate is the captain of your compassion crew, which is here to extend grace and neutralize the harm brought on by the inner critic. Your love advocate will help you come back to love. When shame traps you into condemnation, love and honor will set you free. As you focus on the energy of love, it dissipates the effect of fear, because love is the most powerful force in overcoming fear. I recommend that you search the insight timer app for a loving kindness meditation or listen to *The Love Meditation*[1] on my YouTube channel.

Business Case Unleashed

How companies benefit from helping their employees transform the inner critic to an inner coach (innovation).

In today's dynamic business landscape, fostering innovation is vital for establishing and sustaining a competitive edge. When employees have a harsh inner critic, the organization suffers from stagnation, as it hampers innovation and breeds resistance to change. However, by equipping employees to turn their inner critic into an inner coach, they are more likely to exhibit greater confidence, resilience, and creativity. These qualities form the foundation for fostering invention. This change sets the stage for employees to create new products, services, and processes, positioning the company to outperform competitors and uncover new business opportunities. This contributes to business growth through the development of new revenue streams stemming from these innovative ideas.

4. Deep Breathing

Deep breathing is another way to focus our minds and get out of repetitively dwelling on or rehashing negative thoughts. When we allow ourselves to focus on our breath, it brings us into the present moment. Paying attention to our breath allows our brains to get out of the Default Mode Network (DMN), which is a group of brain regions that can devolve into rumination when we're not in a resourceful place emotionally. The DMN is active when our brain is at rest and not focused on a specific task, but the Task Positive Network (TPN), on the other hand, is activated when the brain is engaged in a specific task. To the degree that the TPN is active, the DMN becomes inactive,[2] which is good news, since focusing on the breath will simultaneously activate the TPN and bring us out of the brooding that happens in the DMN.

In addition to the benefits of activating networks in our brain that will help us get into a brain state that serves us, deep, focused breathing has other effects on our nervous system and bodily functions overall. According to one study by Harvard Medical School,[3] deep breathing can help reduce stress and invoke the relaxation response. The benefits of deep breathing over time can include lower stress levels, which may reduce heart rate and blood pressure, improve immune function, and help manage depression or anxiety.

I've personally found that deep breathing combined with meditation is very helpful in counteracting the stress that comes from the voice of the inner critic. My favorite deep breathing exercise is to inhale from the diaphragm for three counts, hold for one count, and then exhale for six counts. The exhale is double the inhale number because exhaling activates the parasympathetic nervous system, which puts us in a resting state.

5. Self-Care Strategies

Practicing self-care is yet another powerful way to tame the inner critic, as it helps us proactively manage our emotional state. When we take care of ourselves physically, mentally, and spiritually, our emotional resilience is a lot stronger. Simple things can be done routinely to increase one's sense of security, worth, well-being, and inner peace. "These things," as the late Stephen Covey said, "are about sharpening the saw—i.e., preserving and enhancing the greatest asset you have, which is you!"

We all have different ways to sharpen our saw and bring renewal to our lives. Some basic ones are sleep, exercise, and eating well. Beyond the basics, the list is as diverse as our distinct personalities. I love the acronym SAVERS from Hal Elrod's book *The Miracle Morning*[4] to remind me of some of the most effective practices I've incorporated over time. SAVERS stands for Silence (including meditation), Affirmations, Visualization, Exercise, Reading, and Scribing (another way of saying journaling).

6. It's No Biggie

Sometimes we will make mistakes and unwanted things happen—but most of the time, it will be okay. It's usually not that serious, and no one may have even noticed what occurred while we were catastrophizing the situation in our own minds. We need to learn to laugh at ourselves a little more or just shrug something off, knowing it's not a big deal. Learn to release, let go, have fun, and live lighter!

7. Notice and Celebrate Your Successes

The brain's negativity bias causes us to primarily notice and focus on the things we have done wrong. In order to manage our brain's tendency to notice the bad, we have to proactively build neuroplasticity around noticing the good and taking in our positive life experiences. Rick Hanson, a psychologist, author, and teacher who specializes in neuroscience and mindfulness, talks about a process called "taking in the good."[5] This is where we deepen the benefits of positive experiences by noticing them, fully engaging with them, and deliberately integrating them into our being.

Since I'm a writer, journaling is one of the most effective ways for me to focus on and absorb these experiences, as it allows me to be fully present with the words I'm scribing on a page and really feel each emotion as I write them. You, too, can take time to notice the good through journaling or visualizing at the end of your day. When you practice celebrating your wins and noticing the little miracles you encounter daily, you will rewire your brain to focus on your successes. By tilting toward the good, you will bring more happiness and simple joy into your life. Remember this: wherever you spend the majority of your emotional life will determine the level of happiness you have, so intentionally creating more opportunities to "feel the good" will inevitably improve the emotional quality of your life.

We close this chapter with the inner DIVA visualization. We will explore in greater depth in chapter 6 who the DIVA is; for now, just know that she is the savvy woman inside of you that coaches you to:

- *Deliver* results,

- Develop a strong *image* (aka personal brand),

- Get the *visibility* you deserve for your great contributions, and

- Curate a trusted **a**dvisory board that supports you and believes in your potential.

The inner DIVA is your internal coach that guides you to your most resourceful state, where self-doubt loses its power. Your inner DIVA sees the potential you have and calls you up higher. She showers you with love while challenging you to step up into your divine destiny. She will not allow you to shrink back or hide, but like the eagle's mom, she nurtures and teaches you what you're capable of so that you can fly. She helps you on the journey to access who you truly are. The women who go through my Your Power Unleashed coaching program report that this visualization opens them up to new personal revelations that profoundly impact them.

Find a space where you will not be interrupted for twenty minutes and can focus, relax, and keep your eyes closed. Silence your phones and electronic devices, then grab a pen and notebook so that you can journal the insights you receive from your inner coach, the DIVA, when you complete the visualization. I invite you to go to my website (https://www.yourpowerunleashed.org/bookresources) or check the resources section of this book, where you can access a recording of this visualization.

The Inner DIVA Visualization

Close your eyes and take a deep breath in. Relax and breathe.

Allow your mind to go to an exquisite place—the most beautiful place that you've always wanted to be. Where are you? What are your surroundings like? What are the scents, the colors, and the textures that you notice? What sounds do you hear? How does being here make you feel?

Look in front of you—a bit in the distance—and you see a majestic-looking woman walking toward you. What is she wearing? What does she look like? She's getting closer; you can see her face. What's the expression on her face? What is her scent? You look at her, and she looks familiar. She was there with you in the times of your biggest doubts and fears. She supported you. She believed in you. She loved you. She had your back. She was your ride-or-die. You didn't even know it, but she was protecting you even then.

You think of that major obstacle that you went through, and now you realize that she has always been there supporting you, even in what felt like your darkest moments. You're now overwhelmed with gratitude for all she has done for you. She is looking at you with loving kindness, and you begin to show gratitude for her. You thank her for showing up when you needed her most. You didn't know it, but she was there.

You begin to tell her the qualities that she had, for which you were grateful.

1. Thank you for being _____.
2. I am grateful that you are _____.
3. I am grateful that you have always been
_____.

Tell her what these qualities did for you, how they helped you and how her showing up transformed your situation. Tell her that you admire these amazing qualities about her and that you honor and appreciate her and her beautiful, kind heart.

Now picture this DIVA, this queen, in all her royal glory: dignified, majestic, regal, powerful, and beautiful. She says, "Thank you, my love. I'm with you. The me you're seeing is really the truest and most whole part of you. You're healed. You're magnificent. You're whole. You're glorious. You're completely loved. You are brilliance defined. You're a perfect creation. You're whole. Nothing is missing or broken in you. There is nothing wrong with you. You're more than enough. You're powerful. You're stronger than you could ever imagine. You're brave. You are victorious."

Now she tells you, "I want you to repeat after me and say this:
I am _____."

Now, say the first adjective that you thanked her for being at the beginning of this meditation.

Breathe in deeply for three seconds, fully absorbing this word, and exhale slowly for six seconds while you continue to meditate on the word she used to describe you. Own that word. It's one of the truest parts of you.

Again, now she tells you, "I want you to repeat after me and say this:
I am _____."

Now, say the second adjective that you thanked her for being at the beginning of this meditation.
Breathe in deeply for three seconds, fully absorbing this word, and exhale slowly for six seconds while you continue to meditate on the word she used to

describe you. Own that word. It's one of the truest parts of you.

Finally, she tells you, "I want you to repeat after me and say this:
I am _____."

Now, say the third adjective that you thanked her for being at the beginning of this meditation.

Breathe in deeply for three seconds, fully absorbing this word, and exhale slowly for six seconds while you continue to meditate on the word she used to describe you. Own that word. It's one of the truest parts of you.

Then she says, "My dear sister in royalty, remember that I am the real you, your truest self. Every time you need to remember who you truly are, I want you to _____."

Now listen to what she tells you to do to remember.

Then she tells you, "Whenever you need my guidance, I want you to _____."

She now has a special message for you. Listen to the message that she wants you to receive. What is the special message that she shared with you? Deep in your heart, you know this is what you really needed to hear right now. Hold on to this message.

Now, thank her majesty for her wisdom, her words, her love, and her presence. Take a deep breath in and touch the place in your body where you feel her love, then inhale deeply into that place.

Now exhale.

Remember, the DIVA is always with you. She is you!

Now, take three to five minutes to write down what that experience was like for you. What did she tell you? How do you access her? What part of your body can you place your hand on to be reminded of her love? What was the message she gave you? What were the words she used to describe you? Recognize that these admired qualities of your inner coach, the DIVA, are the truest parts of you—the parts of yourself that you've forgotten that are untouched by doubt, limitations, or fear, and the places that you felt like you never really knew but now you do.

I hope this visualization was a transformative experience for you and that you will return to it whenever you need to access your own wisdom and power.

Unleashing the Next Chapter

If you have ever desired to feel the restful assurance that comes from living authentically, to experience a sense of fulfillment because you are completely aligned with your highest priorities, and to uncover a power inside of you that makes you unstoppable in the face of any difficulty, chapter 3 is just for you.

BOLD Actions to Evoke Your Transformation

1. Which of the seven resources will you use in the upcoming week to coach yourself? Block your calendar for seven days to reflect on how the strategy you selected helped you. If you notice minimal benefits, pick another one and try it for a couple of weeks until you find one that works for you.

2. What did you learn from the concept of normalizing and destigmatizing the occurrence of self-doubt? How will you think differently about it based on your new insights from this chapter?

3. What does it mean to you to be aware of your stress response without adopting it as your identity?

4. ***Intersectional reflection question:*** *Which one of the seven coaching resources or the inner DIVA visualization can help you embrace an aspect of who you are (e.g. marital status, skin-tone/color, sexual orientation, national origin) that you have had a complicated relationship with?*

5. What was the experience of doing the inner DIVA visualization like for you? How will the messages that you received during the visualization allow you to coach yourself through self-doubt when it surfaces again?

CHAPTER THREE

VALUES—YOUR ROAD MAP TO FULFILLMENT AND AUTHENTICITY

Live your days on the positive side of life, in tune with your most treasured values. And in each moment, you'll have much to live for.

—*Ralph Marston*

It was past midnight, and my mom opened the gate to allow my dad to drive into the yard. She frantically waved at him to hurry in so that he wouldn't get out of the vehicle to close the gate behind him. She ran back inside the house, and before my dad could register the reason for her strange behavior, he heard two loud gunshots behind him. He quickly ran into the house, grabbed my little sister and me, and hurriedly carried us to the bedroom in the back of our home. I must have been seven years old, unsure of what was happening in the middle of the night or why I was frightened out of my sleep and rushed out of my room. I watched in absolute astonishment as my dad and adult cousin Norma lifted up the 200-pound double dresser filled with clothing and towels over two beds to block the entrance to the room.

Wow, I thought, *they are as strong as Superman!* I still wasn't sure what was going on, but the only thing I thought was that my dad and cousin somehow magically developed herculean strength for thirty seconds. After everything had happened that night, I learned that my dad did all this to protect the lives of his family members during an armed robbery. The men who'd broken in weren't able to get into the sectioned-off part of our home. The crazy thing was that a short while later, when the police officers came to our house, my dad could not lift that dresser again. Everyone had to get in on the action to push it away from the door. He displayed what I now know is called *hysterical strength*, which is a phenomenon where an individual is able to summon extraordinary physical power under extreme emotional distress due to the adrenaline and other hormones released in response to perceived threat or danger. My dad found a big enough reason to fuel him to lift that dresser, something he could never have done without a powerful enough reason.

What if you and I could access energy that would propel us toward our ultimate life purpose, totally unhindered by any obstacle, including fear? What if we could find a powerful enough reason *why* that can energize us to live in alignment with our dreams rather than being paralyzed by fear? What if we could discover fuel inside ourselves that would make us unstoppable in the face of countless obstacles without having to invoke the crisis response of hysterical strength? There is power to do *all* these things and more when we clarify our personal values.

So what are values, exactly? They are the things that we inherently hold as important. These ideologies and priorities that we live by impact everything we do. Understanding our values is one of the most important endeavors we can ever embark upon because our values are our internal compass and drive our every behavior. When we live life honoring our most deeply held values on a daily basis, we tap into a reliable source of fulfillment, peace, joy, and motivation. When we live in a way that disregards or deprioritizes our values, even if we accomplish what may be considered external success, we experience a sense of dissatisfaction and a feeling of being inauthentic or incongruent.

Values empower us to take actions that are in line with our personal priorities because they give us clarity. It's not hard to make decisions when we know what our values are. It's when we're not clear what these priorities are and when we don't make a habit of consistently honoring them that we find ourselves confused about the next step to take. Values work is a practical way we can focus on putting first things first, so that, as Stephen R. Covey said, the things that matter most are never at the mercy of things that matter least.[1] Here are some of the things that values work will help us do:

1. Finding Our Voice: Many times we don't boldly speak up and, as a result, are not viewed as confident communicators, but the root cause of not owning our voice is something else. For instance, sometimes when I'm coaching a client who struggles with expressing themselves or experiences nervousness before a presentation, it often emerges through our sessions that their hesitancy to speak stems from a preoccupation with potential judgment from others about their words or performance, rather than concentrating on the intended message or the purpose of the presentation.

When we take the focus off how we are doing and put it on the purpose or mission that's connected to our own deepest driving values, we find the boldness to use our voices. This is a strategy I use to give myself the confidence to speak with power in my engagements. I do so by envisioning a woman—usually a past or current client to make it real—who has struggled to live up to her own full potential because of fear and doubt. This woman's face re-grounds me in the purpose of my keynote presentation. It reminds me that I don't have to perform like an entertainer, but I'm there to convey a message to someone who desperately needs to be encouraged and be called into her divine destiny. This vision gives me the conviction to speak with power because I'm grounded in my personal values of service and contribution.

2. Establishing Our Own Definition of Success: Many of our fears and the resulting paralysis come from an overemphasis on what others think. We define success according to how other people react to what we do or what they say about us. When we, however, empower ourselves to define success by our own standards, we experience a certain liberation that a client of mine refers to as *internal empowerment*, which allows us to live in alignment with our own purpose. This proactive rather than reactive definition of success allows us to soar freely, since we're no longer shackled by the opinions of other people.

3. Gaining Clarity: As you establish your own definition of success by connecting to your values, you begin to make decisions with greater ease and confidence, which helps you break the habit of second-guessing yourself.

4. Authentic Living: Authenticity and living our truth have become an increasingly common topic in our culture because, in the past, we have overvalued external appearances and tried to keep up with the Joneses but have not found the sense of belonging we were seeking. When we release ourselves from the expectations of others and connect to what is truly important to us, we begin to discover the true self within—what we have spent many years unintentionally burying.

This higher self is able to connect with others on a deeper level as she releases the superficialities that she was once entangled in. It's not so much that we have to find the true self within us; she is already there. It's that we get to discover this powerful person and finally heed her beckoning.

5. Cultivating Executive Presence: In order to get into top jobs and leadership positions, there is a certain "it" factor you're expected to possess. Sylvia Ann Hewlett, in her book *Executive Presence: The Missing Link Between Merit and Success,*[2] states that executive presence is a measure of image: whether you signal to others that you have what it takes and you are star material. Having this quality opens the doors to extraordinary opportunities.

Most ambitious people in the corporate space know that this "it" factor is important but don't really understand what it consists of and what one needs to do to get it. When you live in alignment with your values, there is a certain confidence that comes from being comfortable in your own skin that allows you to project authenticity, poise, and confidence to telegraph to your audience that you're the real thing. We can't telegraph what we don't have; values work helps us connect with and own who we truly are. When we know it and own it, we can project it.

6. Finding Our Mission: Values work primes us for the next phase of our personal development journey, which is finding our deepest mission and purpose. A life driven by purpose can make us virtually unstoppable.

7. Living a Life of Fulfillment: When we live a life honoring our most deeply held values on a daily basis, we tap into a reliable source of fulfillment and motivation.

8. Improving Relationships Through Higher Emotional Quotient (EQ): Values work helps to improve our self-awareness, which is the foundational emotional intelligence (also known as EQ) skill. As we grow in self-awareness and other aspects of EQ, our relationships at work and at home improve. When we understand what other people value and participate in honoring their values with them, they feel connected to us and respected by us. This facilitates empathy and serves as a bridge between them and us. Working on values is, therefore, a powerful way to deepen and strengthen relationships.

Now, let's identify what *your* personal values are.

Activity: Exploring Your Personal Values

When was the last time you accessed your heart's desires? Instead of just asking what your values are, I will engage you in exercises of reflection on stories that have been part of your life experience. Stories bring us into our hearts, where motivation and passion lie, and take us out of our heads. In our minds, a lot of "shoulds" and "ought tos" show up, and they reflect other people's desire for us and society's expectations at large, but they are not a reflection of our deepest personal desires. The following activities will help engage you in your own stories in a meaningful way.

Business Case Unleashed

Helping employees identify their personal values benefits companies (engagement and motivation).

When an organization helps employees identify their personal values, it enables them to take steps to live in alignment with their deepest priorities. This benefits the company because adherence to values fosters a sense of purpose, satisfaction, and fulfillment within employees, which results in increased levels of engagement, motivation, and commitment. This contributes to higher quality output and a more positive work environment. Additionally, employees who feel a strong connection between their personal values and their work are more likely to stay with the company, due to the mission-driven loyalty that comes from this congruence.

Stories One and Two: Values Aligned

Think of a specific experience or event in your life that made you feel very happy and fulfilled. Life seemed to be working in exactly the way you wanted it to. The stars were aligned, so to speak. Visualize one personal example and a professional one. Write down a detailed description of each event, and answer the following questions for each:

- What happened?
- When did this event take place?
- Where were you?
- Who was there?
- What did you do?
- How did this experience make you feel?
- What was the reason you felt this way?

Use the list of values below as a reference to help you identify the ones that appeared in your stories (if there is a value that does not appear on the list, then write it down; this list is just meant to help you get started). Please do this exercise before looking at the list, as you may get distracted by choosing values you think you should have or the ones that sound most appealing. We don't choose our values; we *discover* them. Exercises like this allow us to unveil our true values by digging deep into our hearts rather than allowing our conscious minds to select what we think should be our most important values.

My desire is for you to be liberated from the limits of the "shoulds" that others or society have put upon you. Use these life stories as a tool to uncover your authentic values.

Acceptance	Curiosity	Happiness	Logic	Respect
Achievement	Dedication	Hard work	Love	Responsibility
Adventure	Dependability	Harmony	Loyalty	Resourcefulness
Aesthetics	Determination	Health	Meaningfulness	Results-oriented
Affirmation	Development	Honesty	Nurture	Risk-taking
Authenticity	Discipline	Honor	Nonviolence	Security
Authority	Diversity	Hope	Openness	Selflessness
Balance	Drive	Humanitarianism	Optimism	Self-respect
Beauty	Endurance	Humility	Orderliness	Service
Belonging	Enjoyment	Humor	Originality	Significance
Boldness	Equality	Inclusivity	Ownership	Silence
Bravery	Excellence	Independence	Passion	Simplicity
Candor	Expertise	Individuality	Patience	Solitude
Character	Fairness	Influence	Peace	Spirituality
Collaboration	Faith	Innovation	Pleasure	Spontaneity
Commitment	Family	Inspiration	Popularity	Stability
Community	Fidelity	Integrity	Positivity	Stewardship
Compassion	Follow through	Intelligence	Power	Strength
Competency	Freedom	Joy	Prestige	Success
Confidence	Friendships	Justice	Principled	Status
Connection	Fulfillment	Kindness	Purpose	Structure
Contribution	Fun	Knowledge	Realism	Support
Cooperation	Generosity	Leadership	Recognition	Tenacity
Creativity	Gratitude	Learning	Reliability	Transparency
Credibility	Growth	Legacy	Resilience	Trust

Story Three: Values Violated

Think of another story about an event that was frustrating or disappointing to you. Write down a detailed description of the event. Use the values list as a reference to help you identify the values that were being ignored, disregarded, or stepped on. Here we do a twist on the first exercise, because another powerful way to identify our values is to unpack how it affects us when we're not honoring something that's important to us. The stronger the reaction, the more powerfully we hold the value. You can use the same questions we listed for the first two exercises here as well.

Exercise: Values Lived out or Stepped on by Others

I want you to think of and write down:

- Qualities that you admire most in the people you respect—we admire what we desire

- Qualities that, when you see them lacking in others, really annoy or irritate you

- Qualities that, when you see them present in others, really annoy or irritate you

What Are Your CORE Values?

You now have a list of values that are personally relevant and important to you. How long is this list? If you have a list of more than five values, I invite you to take all your values and rank them in order of importance. The following five classifications will help you rank them:

1. Always valued
2. Often valued
3. Sometimes valued

4. Seldom valued
5. Least valued

The ones that are always valued are your top values. If there are less than five, you can add a few from the often valued ones to determine your top values. Once you've narrowed down your top five values, write them down, memorize them, look at them regularly, and allow these values to become a driving force in your life.

When you live your life honoring these values, you will experience a level of fulfillment that you may have never experienced before because now you're living life on your own terms. You will have a greater feeling of contentment because you've defined what success is to you and will be inspired to live congruently with your truest and highest self. If you allow them to, these values will guide you. They will permit you to make the decisions that are right for you. They will keep you inspired in the face of adversity. They will free you to live as your authentic self, and they will cause you to experience a deeper level of inner peace.

Unleashing the Next Chapter

We frequently spend time trying to fight all the obstacles that are getting in the way of our success, but when we realize that we're often our own biggest enemy, everything changes. Join me in chapter 4 to learn how to stop sabotaging yourself.

BOLD Actions to Evoke Your Transformation

1. What's one thing that you will start doing this week to live in alignment with your core values?
2. What's one thing that you will *stop* doing this week so that you can live more in alignment with your core values? (One thing you can do to keep your top five values top of mind is to print and laminate the list or use it as a screen saver.)

3. At the end of the upcoming week, jot down the key lessons and observations from the actions you took or didn't take to live in alignment with your values. This reflection will help strengthen your understanding.

4. *__Intersectional reflection question:__* Which core value(s) can help you honor parts of yourself e.g. accent, hair type/texture, class/socio-economic status, eye shape, etc. that previously caused shame?

5. Progress is best accomplished in a community, so grab a friend, partner, mentor, or family member that you trust and let them know the actions you've committed to take. Have this person hold you accountable by checking in with you to see if you followed through. A bonus of inviting someone else on this journey with you is that when another person holds space to witness your values and listen to you deeply, it can be an incredibly validating process in a world where we're not customarily supported.

6. If this exercise was helpful for you, I would love to hear your success report. Send me a note at yourpowerunleashed. org/contact to let me know about your experience with the exercises, or send me a message on LinkedIn via my name, Kisha Wynter.

CHAPTER FOUR

STOPPING FEAR-DRIVEN SELF-SABOTAGE

*Our deepest fear is not that we're inadequate. Our deepest
fear is that we're powerful beyond measure.*

—*Marianne Williamson*

I worked in Compensation and Benefits for more than seven years
at one of the companies most respected for their HR function. It
blew my mind that someone with my background—the daughter
of two people who never graduated from college and who worked
blue-collar jobs all their lives—could have a corporate job, her
own office, and a decent salary that afforded her the ability to
provide for herself, including buying a home before the age of
twenty-seven. From the outside looking in, life was good— in
fact, very good—but internally, I was miserable.

Although I was comfortable in my position, I was bored out
of my mind. I thought, *There has to be more.*

As I sat at my desk getting ready to launch the salary planning
season for the sixth year in a row, I felt a wave of anxiety wash
over my body, and I thought, *I cannot do this for another year.*

The very thought of going through this process again made
my head pound and gave me a nauseated feeling in my stomach.

I knew I had to do something; otherwise, this anxiety I felt would consume me. As you read this, you may wonder why I didn't just look for another job. But it wasn't that simple. The truth is, I knew the exact job I wanted and had applied for it a couple of years earlier, but I was ignored. I never even got a call back. I was rejected, and my ego was hurt. Sometimes we want to make a change that will catapult us right into our heart's desires, but we allow fear to stop us from stepping up. The fear of being rejected all over again and the fear of failing at a brand-new role brought me to a standstill. If I could've mustered up the courage, it would have become the bridge filling the distance between the current level of achievement I was experiencing and fully manifesting the potential I was destined to step into.

I wanted to find a role that didn't just pay the bills but one that made my heart sing instead of race, as it was doing at that moment. In my heart, I already knew what that role was, and every year, I wrote down the same role I wanted in my annual performance review. By the same token, every year except for one, I did absolutely nothing about this desire. The one year I made a feeble attempt to go after the role, I didn't succeed, so I retreated. I'm embarrassed by my lack of tenacity to just go for it. I allowed fear of failure and rejection to paralyze me. Yet, I knew that on that specific day, as I was about to launch into another salary planning season, I had to do something. I could not continue like this.

So I searched the internal career system, and just by luck, I found the perfect role. I printed the job description and quickly ran to my boss's office to show it to him before I could talk myself out of applying to it. I figured if I told him, I wouldn't be able to back out. I was surprised by his swift reaction. I expected him to say, as so many others had over the years, that I didn't have experience in this area and "we can't afford to lose you."

Instead, he looked at the description and said, "Oh, you can totally do this role. Do you want me to call the hiring manager now?"

I said, "Right now? No, it's okay. You're busy. You don't have to call them."

Ignoring my protests, he immediately placed a call, and within five minutes, an interview was scheduled. Just like that, the trajectory of my career changed! I got the job and excelled in it for a couple of years, which prepared me for bigger roles more aligned with my career aspirations. As they say, the rest is history.

That ultimately led me to my life's work in leadership development and executive coaching. As I followed the path to release fear and break out of self-sabotaging patterns, one opportunity after another opened up for me—from leading initiatives in the organization, to designing programs, to coaching, and then to speaking opportunities, which gave me the experience and confidence I needed to start my own consulting practice. I learned that my secret to success was to allow myself to feel the fears that came up for me yet go after what I wanted anyway without shrinking back.

Most of us have a consistent set of sabotage patterns that we go back to over and over again when we're afraid. One of my patterns was shrinking back from big opportunities where I was sure I would fail. If I thought I could find a way to figure out how to do something, I was all in, but if I thought it was too big for me, I would shrink back. If I had not broken my pattern of self-sabotage when fear arose, I would not be where I am today, doing what I love and living my purpose and mission.

Let me ask you this: What would your life look like if you had the courage to fully step up and go after your heart's desire? Not what you feel comfortable or secure doing, but the thing that would make your heart sing. If you're like me, you probably already know what that thing is. Or maybe you don't—that's fine too. Either way, let's look at some ways in which you could be sabotaging your own progress and explore behaviors you can adopt that will break that pattern.

Self-Sabotage

Self-sabotage is when we take actions or don't take important actions, and it gets in the way of our success. Most people don't get up in the morning with the intention of deliberately blocking their own progress. What happens is that they fear change and will work ferociously to stay inside their comfort zone, where they mistakenly think they're safe. Fear activates the survival mechanism of the fight-or-flight response, and this self-protection causes self-sabotage.

Fear shows up in many different ways for each person, so the list of possible fears that get in the way of our success is endless. Let's be honest, it feels good to dream and to set goals because when we engage in these activities, it gives us a boost of dopamine, the feel-good neurotransmitter. However, when it's time to actually execute, our enemy, fear, triggers behaviors that drive us to avoid the actions necessary to attain the goals we've set.

In this section, we will explore the various manifestations of fear, and then we will explore common ways in which people sabotage their progress. As we go through the upcoming section, I invite you to think about which of these ways is part of your normal self-sabotage pattern. Here's the good news: self-awareness is the first step to breaking the pattern. Once we have shed light on these trends, I will share strategies on how to overcome them.

Part I: Manifestations of Fear

1. Fear of Failure or Success:

Many of us are familiar with a very common manifestation of fear—the fear of failure. We know that we fear failure because we don't want to look bad in front of others and perhaps even confirm our own fears of not being good enough. What we're less familiar with is the fear of success. People fear success because of the responsibility that comes with it, or the visibility. They also fear success because they're not sure they can maintain it or repeat the actions they took to get there. If they aren't able to do it again, it could mean disappointing themselves or the expectations of people who hold them in high regard.

When I worked at GE, I had an associate who won an award in her first year of the company's prestigious leadership development program, Corporate Audit Staff. This was an award that only the top 1 percent won, and if they did, it would be in their second or third year. But this person, whom I will call Felicia, won the award within her first year in the organization. She immediately got the attention of leaders not only across the department but across the entire company, and there was immediate talk of her runway to the executive ranks. My custom at that time as an HR leader was to do regular one-on-one coaching sessions with employees, and as I kicked off our discussion, I congratulated her.

The response she gave me took me by surprise. She stated that she was terribly scared that she would not live up to everyone's expectations and feared that she could not do excellent work like this again. She felt the heavy load of high expectations from her leaders and wanted things to go back to how they were before, in the safety of not being seen or known and playing under the radar.

The coaching I gave her is the strategy I will give you here. If you succeed at something, take the time to reflect on the process that led to that success. This may mean analyzing both the mental habits that allowed you to play big rather than small and the work habits that led to your achievements, then documenting them so that you can focus on things that you can control that are repeatable. Become a student of both your successes and failures. Change the definition of success from getting the award, losing weight, or any other outcomes; and allow success to be defined as your commitment to the actions you took to get there, as well as the lessons you learned along the way.

In Felicia's case, for example, some of the things she did that led to her huge success were spending a lot of extra time talking to previous teams that worked in the area, reviewing all their prior analysis and documentation, not being afraid to ask the tough questions of senior leaders, and getting perspectives from the clients they were serving on what worked well with prior teams and what didn't.

I told her to focus on these things that led to the award rather than being concerned about whether or not she could get the award again. These success habits were repeatable and totally within her control, but getting the award wasn't within her power.

I propose that you adopt the same strategy of focusing on the actions that lead to *your* success, because they are totally within your control, and quit worrying about the outcome, something over which you have little control.

Ironically, when you focus on the actions that it takes to get the result, you often end up getting that outcome anyway, but with less stress. Trust that as long as you focus on taking the right actions and look at any failure as a learning opportunity to tweak your strategy, the results will eventually come. Failure is just part of the learning process that will get you to the point of winning and thriving if you remain consistent in following through.

2. Fear of Rejection

According to Abraham Maslow's hierarchy of needs, we have a need to belong, and belonging is a major source of human motivation. The fear of rejection is a direct threat to this need to belong. Feeling rejected can feel painful and may even remind us of trauma related to rejection in various periods of our lives. The effort to avoid rejection can lead to some distinct self-sabotaging patterns. If you were criticized by caretakers, abandoned by a parent, or experienced bullying in your life, rejection may be a particular challenge for you. If you're dealing with the fear of rejection, here are some simple things you can do to keep moving through the fear and not let it paralyze you from taking action.

The first step is to acknowledge that you experience trepidation regarding being rejected and accept this feeling as a natural part of the human experience. Don't make yourself wrong for feeling the way you do. Validating instead of shaming yourself for your internal reactions will allow you to build emotional resilience and self-compassion and promote the adoption of healthier coping strategies. When dealing with the stressors that come from fear, many of us try to suppress or ignore them, but this does not work and just intensifies the effect of the stress on our brains and nervous system. Instead of suppressing the fear and the associated shame we have for feeling it, it's more beneficial to name the emotions that are surfacing. When we name our emotions rather than suppress them, this is very effective, because the research[1] from psychologist and neuroscientist Lisa Feldman Barrett shows that the more granular we can get about the emotions we're experiencing, the more we will lower the physiological toll of the stress on our bodies.

Once we specify the emotion, the next step is to remove the shame associated with it by recognizing that the need to belong is a basic human need; therefore, be gentle with yourself for fearing rejection. This will help you normalize and destigmatize it. Once you normalize the apprehension, decide to do what you're afraid of regardless of how you currently feel so that you can build new experiences that you can draw upon to show you that people will reject you much less than you imagine. This evidence gathered from real-world experiences that you're creating will be a powerful source to draw upon whenever self-doubt begins to plague you.

I really enjoyed the TED Talk by Jia Jiang, titled "What I Learned from 100 Days of Rejection,"[2] because he talked about the experiences he had when he took the risk of asking for what he wanted despite the fear he felt and all the wonderful opportunities that opened up for him as a result of staying in action. He realized that many things he feared were simply not true and would never happen.

I believe that as you embark on acting despite fear, you, too, will find that many of the things you were afraid of are also not real.

3. Fear of Criticism

Being criticized is an unpleasant experience, but it's inevitable if you want to play big. If your actions in the world are significant, you will draw detractors. Imagine the well-known people in the world whom you love and admire. Now, think about all the people who have something negative to say about them. A scroll through their social media will give you all the information you need. Here's the reality: anyone who's doing things that make a difference or that have a transformational impact will open themselves up to being criticized, especially by those who are not busy doing impactful things themselves.

Aristotle is quoted as saying, "There is only one way to avoid criticism: do nothing, say nothing, and be nothing." Once you realize and accept that critics don't matter, you can shift your focus to your personal mission and values, which are powerful driving forces. I once allowed myself to be aggravated by a man who misinterpreted my empowering message to women as being anti-men when, in fact, I never once mentioned men in my message. He had some preconceived notion that any discussion about female empowerment would somehow devolve into male-bashing. I knew this wasn't my intention, but I wasted energy listening to what he was saying and allowing myself to be irritated by it. I rebounded by focusing on all the women who had gone through my coaching program and whose lives were forever changed as a result of the work I did.

As I reflected, I realized that my value of contributing to people's lives and helping them live up to their full potential made the criticism of one random guy irrelevant because my *purpose* was clear. He was not part of my target audience; however, if a significant subset of my target audience provided me with feedback about something that didn't resonate with them, it would have been wise for me to engage in a conversation with those for whom I hoped my work would benefit so that I could elevate my impact. Whenever someone criticizes us in a constructive way, especially if we have a valued relationship with them, I believe that we should listen.

I try to ask myself, "What is the lesson here? Do I just dismiss it, or is there an opportunity to tweak my strategy so that my message or intention isn't misinterpreted? If I change my strategy, will it allow me to influence the audience more effectively?"

Criticism can be converted into helpful lessons that can accelerate our growth and learning by revealing blind spots, if we learn to receive them from the *right* people without taking them personally.

4. Fear of Danger

There's a saying I love and remind myself of regularly: 99 percent of the things we worry about never happen. Remember what I shared with you in chapter 1, that the primary function of the brain is to keep us safe? Fear messages are the brain's attempt to do just that. However, when we develop the ability to perceive beyond the surface-level conversations happening in the brain, we will realize that there is more going on. Ask yourself: What message is the anxiety from fear trying to bring me? Is it that I need to spend more time preparing beforehand? If you fear health issues or financial danger, have you done all you can to take care of your body, or have you saved, budgeted, and invested financially?

In her book *The Language of Emotions: What Your Feelings Are Trying to Tell You*,[3] author Karla McLaren shares helpful insights about the emotion of fear and how it carries hidden messages, which she calls gifts. If we slow down and pay attention, I know from personal experience that we can receive the gift(s) found in our emotions, including the gift of fear. According to McLaren, fear may signal a need for more preparation, readiness, attentiveness, and focus. The bottom line is that fear of danger might be a signal to do something that will preempt potential negative outcomes. It helps us test the situation we're experiencing realistically and focus on pragmatic actions to take that will address it.

Fear, as with all other emotions, comes to give us a message, and instead of aggressively trying to resist the message or suppress it, which you already know doesn't work, we need to be present with it, listen to the message that it's trying to bring us, process it, and then gently release it. This is how we allow fear to move through and out of us rather than being stuck by it and in it.

Part II: Ways We Sabotage Our Progress or Success

A few years ago, I asked a question at a personal development workshop for entrepreneurs and executives that I was attending about how to deal with the overwhelm I was experiencing. Instead of answering my question, the speaker asked me, "How long have you been using overwhelm as a strategy to sabotage your progress?"

I looked at her, stunned. It felt like she'd slapped me in the face. I had never made the connection that overwhelm was a pattern that I'd developed that slowed down or sometimes halted my ability to take forward-moving action. She went on to describe how people used overwhelm as an excuse, which hindered their progress. After that discussion, I started paying attention to other ways people I worked with in coaching, as well as myself, got in their own way.

Below are some of the common sabotage mechanisms that I've discovered. Which one of these rings true for you? Are there any other patterns that get in the way of your progress that I haven't listed?

Overwhelm

When we're overwhelmed, we allow the feeling of having too much to do completely overpower us so that we stop moving forward. This is a particular struggle for us as women because we frequently take on a lot of tasks in an attempt to prove ourselves and our worthiness through massive workloads. These unrealistic workloads can lead to burnout, which was exactly what my client in chapter 1 was experiencing because she was still trying to prove to her mother who had passed away that she wasn't lazy. Burnout can result in paralysis or your health forcing you to slow down. You will realize a theme with all of these sabotage mechanisms—their effect is to delay or completely stop us from moving forward. As I'm typing this, I'm even more keenly aware of how these feelings destroy our chances of success because their impact is to stop us from doing the very things that will make us win. This includes setting boundaries and saying no when it's appropriate.

What you'll need to do to conquer overwhelm is to transmute it into momentum. Overwhelm causes stagnation, but the right action ignites momentum. You win when you move forward despite your feelings, when you keep going and don't stop. The way to keep going when overwhelm emerges is to break down the big task into one very small and manageable microaction. You will then take the action, then take the next one, and the next one until you gain momentum. However, in order to take action on the right thing that fuels momentum, you must have the courage to also say no to distractions and obligations that don't align with your goals.

Ruminating/Overthinking

Ruminating and overthinking are other mechanisms that come up for many of my clients. I love to point out to anyone who struggles with this that they are great meditators because ruminating, overthinking, and worrying are just meditating on the bad things that could happen rather than focusing on the good. In other words, overthinking is simply a harmful form of meditation. The way to break through rumination is to replace thinking with action because, from a neuroscience standpoint, our brains will not stay in rumination when we are in action.

In chapter 2, we explored how the Task Positive Network (TPN) in the brain is activated through focused deep breathing, which puts our brain in a state of increased parasympathetic activity and reduced stress response. Ann Betz, an expert in the neuroscience of human consciousness, dives deeper into the power of being able to intentionally access these brain networks in her blog.[4] She explains that the Default Mode Network (DMN) and the TPN, two distinct neural networks in the brain, have an inverse or seesaw relationship. Remember, the DMN is a network of brain regions that is active when the individual is not focused on the outside world and the brain is in wakeful rest. It's called default because it's the network that's activated *unless* we're specifically engaged in a goal-directed activity and external input, the realm of the TPN. One of the most interesting aspects of these two networks goes back to the nature of their inverse relationship: to the degree Default is active, Task is not; and to the degree Task is active, Default is not.

If you didn't catch this in her quote, Betz is explaining that the Default Mode Network, where we daydream or ruminate, cannot be active at the same time we're engaged in a goal-directed activity (the domain of the TPN). This means that by just taking action toward our goal, we will switch off rumination and overthinking! My coach, Lisa Nichols, says, "Action is the antidote for despair."

It really is that simple: take action, and you will stop overthinking!

Disorganization

You might be surprised to see that disorganization shows up on the list of sabotage strategies, but it's here because anything that gets in the way of, disrupts, or undermines success is sabotage. Disorganization can be a major hindrance to reaching your goals, and it may be due to several reasons. Think about which one of these applies to you. Disorganization can be caused by having too much to do, more than likely because you have a hard time saying no to others, whether it's being unwilling to have the difficult conversation, or being people-pleasing. Having too much on your plate can result in a lack of focus, so ask yourself if the reason you cannot keep up is because you have an unrealistic workload. Do you find yourself taking on everything instead of daring to speak up for yourself and for your own needs? Don't avoid hard things—advocate for yourself. This quote by author and codependency expert Claudia Black helps motivate me to say no when I need to: "Saying no can be the ultimate self-care."

Indecisiveness and Confusion

Indecisiveness and confusion are two additional ways that people self-sabotage. Indecisiveness comes from doubting that we're taking the right step, which leads to fear. It could be fear of making a mistake by choosing the wrong option, so we choose not to decide. We might be afraid of facing the consequences of a hard choice, whether it's disappointing someone or having to have a conversation we don't want to have. However, if we magnify the core value that drives us and center ourselves on that powerful value, it can be powerful enough to break us free from fear. I know that when I go back to my core value of contribution, it helps me make a hard choice that propels me forward, even if the task ahead is not easy.

The following words from Marianne Williamson, taken from her book *A Return to Love: Reflections on the Principles of A Course in Miracles,*[5] help ground me in my desire to help others and remind me of a mission that's greater than myself. She says, "As we let our own light shine, we unconsciously give other people permission to do the same. As we're liberated from our own fear, our presence automatically liberates others."

This simple quote moves me to make a decision, knowing that the courage to do this can set off a ripple effect of inspiration that will call others upward to also be brave themselves. Can you see how this is a powerful inspiration to step up and make a bold choice if you value contributing to the lives of others in an impactful way? Do you have a quote that can help ground you in your core values and inspire you to take action aligned with them? If you don't have such a centering quote, I encourage you to find one.

> **Business Case Unleashed**
> *Corporations benefit when employees stop self-sabotaging (employee well-being and stress management).*
> Addressing fear-driven self-sabotage among employees is not only crucial for their individual success but also holds significant implications for the overall health of the company. By providing support to help employees overcome these obstacles, the organization can directly impact their mental and emotional well-being, leading to reduced stress and increased satisfaction among the workforce. This, in turn, contributes to a healthier work environment, ultimately fostering a culture of resilience and well-being within the company. Helping employees in this way demonstrates strong commitment to the workforce and has the potential to yield additional long-term benefits.

Rigidity

Rigidity is the opposite of disorganization and is also a sabotage mechanism. In order to explain the impact of rigidity, let's talk about the hemispheres of the brain. When the left hemisphere of the brain is in a resourceful place, it brings structure to the table, which gives us order and clarity on the next steps and helps us develop a step-by-step process to achieve our goals. Structure allows us to feel in control and on target. When we're triggered by a stressor, the left hemisphere can go into an unresourceful state to try to regain control of the situation, which moves the brain from structure to rigidity.

Rigidity is structure taken to the extreme and is a stress response due to fear. Think of a person who is very rigid and resists change with intensity. If you probe further, it's because they are very afraid of something bad happening, so they become rigid to ensure that all the precautionary actions are taken in the hopes of preventing a bad thing from happening.

A perfect example of fear-driven rigidity comes from a movie I saw, *Everything, Everything*, where the main character, Maddy, lived in an extremely sanitized home where her mother never allowed her to leave the house because she supposedly has SCID, severely combined immunodeficiency. Maddy lived a very restricted life where she was cut off from the outside world. After a series of events, she learned that she didn't have SCID but that her mom constructed this extremely rigid life for Maddy after losing her son and husband in a horrible car accident. Since Maddy was the only person her mother had left in the world, she was so scared of losing her that she created this false diagnosis to keep her away from a dangerous world. Maddy was robbed of so many life experiences because of her mother's fear of losing her.

Fear can cause us to be obsessive, controlling, and inflexible, which are characteristics of rigidity. Can you think of times when you were so scared of a negative outcome that you became inflexible and controlling? Remember that structure and order are good, but rigidity is an unhelpful fear-driven response.

Shrinking or Playing Small

I've found three main reasons why people shrink or play small. The first is because they haven't owned their brilliance. These people struggle with a lack of confidence because they haven't taken stock of how much they have contributed to the success of an organization or acknowledged the impact they've made. If we don't recognize the positive effect of our own work and validate ourselves as a result, it will be hard to sustain high self-worth over time. This is why it's important to develop a practice of self-affirmation and to catch ourselves winning.

The second reason is due to the desire to display humility, which may have come from societal or cultural influences. Many of us have had parents who taught us the importance of being humble or, if you're like me, you learned the importance of this in a religious institution like the church. I've met people from various Asian cultures who place a high value on humility, where talk of your own accomplishments is viewed as bragging. Jackson Lu, an assistant professor of work and organization studies at MIT Sloan, led a study on why East Asians are underrepresented in leadership positions[6] in the US and found that East Asian cultures emphasize humility and conformity over assertiveness and that this cultural mismatch between East Asian norms of communication and what American companies hold as ideals in leadership style plays a big role in this inequality.

Although I believe the ultimate solution is for US companies to expand their view of how a leader should behave to be more inclusive instead of the current narrow prototype, there is also value in internally owning one's contribution and being careful not to dismiss or undervalue it.

The third reason people shrink or play small is because of a fear of how others may perceive and respond to their achievements. One such phenomenon is what's called the Tall Poppy Syndrome in Australia and New Zealand, which is a social tendency to belittle those who are viewed as having attained too much success. These people are criticized so that they can be cut down to the size of everyone else around them.

In my own Jamaican culture, we refer to it as "crabs in a barrel," where society drags you back down if you aim too high and achieve what is viewed as too much success, lest "yuh tink yuh betta dan dem" (translation: you think you're better than they are). These are all methodologies that society constructs to prevent disruption of the status quo. These two illustrations are examples of how the wounding of *diminishment* from *the criticized child* I talked about in chapter 1 manifests in different cultures.

Procrastination

Procrastination is an obvious form of self-sabotage, as we know that when we put off tasks, it can result in missed deadlines, missed opportunities, and increased stress levels. We do this because we're avoiding the discomfort of engaging in actions that we don't like but that prevent us from attaining our goals when we put them off. The best way to get out of the procrastination cycle is to break down the big action into more manageable, bite-sized steps and enlist the help of accountability partners to get you there. One of my favorite strategies to stop procrastinating is to set my timer for five minutes and commit to doing a task for just a few minutes. Once the five minutes is up, I give myself permission to stop, but most of the time, once I start, I just want to keep going.

Part III: Behaviors to Break Self-Sabotage

Now that I've defined the various ways in which we sabotage ourselves, the next step is to identify strategies that will facilitate our ability to consistently move toward our goals.

1. Take Small, Consistent Action Now, and Do So Before You Feel Ready!

We fall into overwhelm when we contemplate everything that needs to be done in order to accomplish our big goals; in doing so, we overlook the powerful momentum that taking small, consistent action can create. One key example is when I was a mid-distance runner. I was always the person who had to go big or go home. This would manifest itself in my striving to do the ninety-minute run or the two-hour workout. The challenge was that when my work schedule was super busy, I would do nothing for a week, which resulted in sporadic and inconsistent fitness levels.

On the other hand, I noticed that my consistently fit friends would work out for an hour daily, but when their schedules didn't allow for long workouts, they never stopped, even if it was just twenty or thirty minutes. Due to their consistent small actions, they never lost momentum.

The other important aspect to consider is that people like this would not wait until they felt ready to get started; they would just start with a small step and build competency over time. They didn't wait to feel ready because they knew that feelings were temperamental, and chances are, if you wait until you feel ready, you never will be.

Perfectionism causes many of us to wait until all conditions are perfect and every qualification is fulfilled before we take action, but the problem is that people like this never feel as if they've arrived. However, when we start small and keep going, we create a snowball effect of progress, and eventually, the feelings catch up. The people who succeed just take consistent, imperfect actions.

2. Determine Your Daily Top Three

Back in 2020, I started following a creative content strategist, Erin White, who shared on her YouTube channel, *Erin on Demand*,[7] how much of a procrastinator she was and that she started experimenting with determining a daily top three to overcome procrastination. It seemed like a simple way to take small steps toward my own goals every day, so I joined her in this experiment and found it easy to implement. The strategy is to identify three tasks you must complete on a particular day and focus your energy on completing them. Once you complete the three tasks, it's a major win, so celebrate yourself and then move on to any other additional tasks you have.

3. Learn to Prioritize, Delegate, or Eliminate

Whenever there are a lot of things on your plate, I've found it helpful to put them into categories in order to make the to-do list more manageable. The first category is determining which item on the list is the priority, meaning that it's one of the most important things you need to do in order to achieve your goal. Once you prioritize the list, you can determine which items you need to do and which ones you can delegate to someone else. A lot of people think that they have to do something for it to get done, when in fact, many tasks can and should be done by someone else so that we can free up our time to focus on the tasks that only we can do, the items that require our skill and are in our zone of genius. Anything else that's left that's not a priority can be delayed until another time or completely eliminated.

4. Adopt the Pareto Principle (80/20 rule)

The Pareto principle, also known as the 80/20 rule, is another way to ensure that you're putting the first things first. It states that 80 percent of results come from 20 percent of the inputs or causes. The principle suggests that a majority of outcomes are driven by a relatively small number of factors. If you are a salesperson, for example, 80 percent of your revenue may come from 20 percent of your customers, so the most prudent strategy would be to focus your efforts on cultivating a relationship with this small group of people. You will need to ascertain what the key 20 percent effort is that you need to make in your field or area of focus that will yield 80 percent of the results.

5. Take a Break and Come Back Fresh

Sometimes, when we feel overwhelmed by a task and can't think clearly about what the next best step should be, it's a sign that we need to take a break. Have you ever tried to solve a problem and just could not figure it out, then decided to do something else, like going for a walk or taking a shower, and when you least expected it, boom, the solution came? This is the amazing shift that comes when you allow your brain to take a break from having such a hard time focusing on getting the right answer or solution.

When you step away, you allow your mind to relax or roam, and the answer shows up when you least expect it. You may need a break to step away for a few hours or a couple of days to allow the right strategy to come to you. Be careful, though, that you don't allow this short break to be extended and slip into procrastination sabotage.

6. What Would Your Inner DIVA Tell You to Do?

Sometimes you will need an inspirational push to help you take the first step as you face delayed action. The inner DIVA visualization that you did in chapter 2 can serve as this powerful inspiration. In the visualization, you received words that described the character of your truest self. You received a way to access the wisdom that lies within. Go back and review the journal entries you made from this visualization so that you can get back in touch with this inner wisdom that will guide you to the inspired action that's right for you to take now. Do the visualization again if you need to.

7. Learn to Trust Yourself

One of my primary motivations for designing the inner DIVA visualization is that you will use it as a vehicle to inspire you to trust yourself. Sometimes you will have all the strategies from research given by renowned experts, but based on your own inner wisdom, unique life experiences, and training, your intuition leads you to another path. Learn to trust that voice within, for it holds the answers you seek. As we learn to have faith in our instincts from the knowledge we've acquired in our life's journey, we will begin to unleash the power within and make a profound impact on the world that surrounds us.

8. Write Down Your Goals, and Track Your Progress Weekly with an Accountability Partner

A study by Dr. Gail Matthews,[8] a psychology professor at the Dominican University of California, shows that when you write down your goals and dreams on a daily basis, you become 42 percent more likely to achieve them than those who don't write them down. What is not frequently cited in this study is that if you write down these goals and send them to a friend weekly, you are 178 percent more likely to achieve them! The best way to maintain action as you break through self-sabotage is to write down your goals, create an action plan to attain them, and find an accountability partner with whom you will check in on a weekly basis to ensure that you stay on track.

9. Determine the Worst-Case Scenario and Create a Contingency Plan

If, by the unlikely chance, you tried every tactic and are still paralyzed from taking action, allow yourself to follow the fear. Suppressing fear does not work long term, so embrace it. Play out the worst-case scenario and consider what the consequences will be, both immediate and long term, as well as the impact. Once you've done so, brainstorm potential actions you can take in each worst-case scenario. Think about the strategies you could use to address it, the resources you have available to you, and any alternative action you can take to mitigate the impact. Once you play out the worst case and realize that you still have what it takes to overcome it, even the worst case will not feel as debilitating to you.

Unleashing the Next Chapter

Life experiences have caused us to construct false selves as survival mechanisms and resulted in us forgetting the marvel of who we truly are. The practices in chapter 5 will help you remember who you were before the weight of the world obscured your true essence. They will guide you in unlocking your limitless potential as you uncover the mysterious miracle that lies within. Let's go meet your true self, the Bold Audacious Courageous You.

BOLD Actions to Evoke Your Transformation

Although breaking the habit of self-sabotage can be difficult, it's worth the effort, and in this chapter, you learned all the strategies needed to make significant progress. Here are the BOLD Actions that you should take to ensure your progress:

1. Identify which manifestation of fear commonly affects your ability to take action. Remember, it could be the fear of success, rejection, criticism, or danger.

2. Which is the top way you tend to sabotage your success?

3. Which behaviors to break self-sabotage will you try in the upcoming week? Whichever one you choose, I encourage you to use tactic number 8 to support your success by finding an accountability partner to whom you will send weekly updates about your progress.

4. ***Intersectional reflection question:*** *Is there an aspect of your identity (e.g., race, religion, indigenous identity, gender identity) that has contributed to a fear for your safety or of being criticized and rejected? What's a small action that you can take to give you a sense of empowerment and control?*

CHAPTER FIVE

CULTIVATING BAC (THE BOLD, AUDACIOUS, COURAGEOUS YOU)!

*Every action you take is a vote for the type of person you
wish to become. No single instance will transform your
beliefs, but as the votes build up, so does the evidence of
your new identity.*

—James Clear

Just one more mile to go, I thought. It felt as if my legs were about
to give out, but surprisingly, after running nine miles in the rain,
I was not gasping for air. I had never run this far or this long in
my entire life. This race was an incredible feat for me, considering
my history as a child asthmatic. I felt immense pride as I thought
about what a significant milestone this was—completing my very
first race. Asthma had plagued me throughout my childhood, and
it wasn't until I reached the age of twenty-two that I finally experienced full healing.

Half of my life had been spent grappling with this ailment, enduring hospital stays where I lay in bed for days getting treatment
(which I thought was oxygen) to open my airways and improve
my breathing. You can probably imagine that the fear of being
out of breath haunted me, causing me to shy away from activities that might trigger an asthma attack. The idea of becoming a

runner, though I desired it, as any Jamaican child would, seemed like an unattainable dream.

As I entered the working world, however, I was surrounded by running enthusiasts, and as destiny would have it, I worked for a manager and teammates who weren't just casual joggers or even sprinters, but freaking marathoners! My childhood desire to run was reignited, and luckily, by this time, I no longer had asthma. I felt left out of the workplace excitement of race preparation and events, so one day, I decided to join in. True to my nature, I jumped headfirst into the world of long-distance running without much thought or planning.

As I prepared for this race, I went from couch potato to ten-mile runner in eight weeks flat. It was not a wise decision, I know, but it was definitely in line with my all-or-nothing personality. During that intense eight-week period, I knew that I had to begin seeing myself as a runner if I would ever make it to and through race day. This was a challenging perspective, as I still saw myself through the lens of my past—an asthmatic who couldn't run.

To facilitate this mental transformation, I immersed myself in running-related content. I devoured books, blogs, and articles about running; watched movies and documentaries themed around the sport; and engaged in daily conversations regarding running with my boss and colleagues. I also spent a considerable amount of time exploring and purchasing running gear from upscale running stores in my neighboring town of Greenwich, Connecticut. I don't know why, but this particular action of being in these fancy running stores made me feel as if I was on my way to becoming an elite runner.

But above all, I ran. I ran almost every single day. With each run, every time I laced up my running shoes, I felt less like an asthmatic and more like a runner. This consistent action enabled me to reprogram my mind's perception of who I was, effectively rewiring how I saw myself.

Although this race tested my perseverance, when I passed mile nine and a half, I felt excited because I knew the finish line was near. I saw my mom's face on the sidelines and could tell she had been anxiously waiting for me. It seemed as if I would not be the last person to finish the race, but a tenacious woman who appeared to be in her seventies was hot on my heels.

I thought, *I know this is my first race, but I will be damned if I, a thirty-one-year-old, will let someone forty-plus years my senior beat me.*

My ego would definitely not tolerate this. Under different circumstances, she would have been an inspiration to me, proof that age was no barrier to achievement, but in this moment, don't be fooled; she *was* my competition. She managed to overtake me. But with every last ounce of energy and determination within me, I summoned a final burst of effort and surged past her. Crossing the finish line just seconds ahead, I secured a second-to-last position. The feeling of elation washed over me as I realized that my placement didn't matter—I had completed the race, defying my own doubts about my endurance. Not only that, but I was also able to breathe, as simple as that sounds, for a former asthmatic; breathing is everything. That day marked a turning point for me. Over the next five years, I completed six half-marathons, fully embracing my identity as a runner. That initial race was more than just a physical achievement; it sparked a profound transformation in how I saw myself. Running became my pathway to breaking free from the limiting beliefs I held. Little did I know that each stride was helping me shed my false self, paving the way for a deeper sense of authenticity and self-discovery.

False Self Concepts

In chapter 2, I introduced the concept of the false self as personas we create to protect ourselves from the challenging experiences we have endured. These identities serve as survival strategies, but we often mistakenly perceive them as our true self. Consequently, we find ourselves trapped in roles that hinder us from living the life we truly want and prevent us from realizing our full potential.

How we view ourselves can be influenced by passively accepting the labels imposed upon us or by reacting defensively to how others see us. Alternatively, we can proactively discover our true self through intentional action and reflection.

A False Self #1: *Labeliedentity* – Accepting Labels

I created "*Labeliedentity*" as a play on the words *label, lie,* and *identity* to describe the concept of embracing false identities shaped by the labels imposed upon us by others.

Labeliedentity is an identity based on a lie, where we believe in, accept, and internalize the labels other people assign to us. We are born into the world as blank slates, and as babies, we really have no idea who we are. Therefore, we look to our parents and to those in our community to reflect to us who we should be. These imposed identities (the true impostors) are accepted without question, primarily due to our lack of self-knowledge and early conditioning, especially when we are fed these lies at a young age. Unfortunately, as discussed in chapter 1, this is accompanied by the internalized wounding of the criticized child because of the judgment, shame, or diminishment we experienced at a young age. *Labeliedentity* often results in us forming our sense of self based on these life experiences, leading to a distorted self-perception and a constant search for external validation and direction.

The impact of *labeliedentity* is that it can hinder personal growth and self-actualization by limiting our ability to explore our authentic selves. It may result in a lack of self-confidence, self-acceptance, and a diminished sense of personal agency.

In professional settings, *Labeliedentity* may manifest as self-doubt, where we feel inadequate or undeserving of our accomplishments due to this internalized false identity. This can undermine career advancement, hinder creativity and innovation, and lead to difficulties in building authentic professional relationships.

A False Self #2: *Pridentity* – Reacting to How Others See Us

This is an identity created by our ego to prove to others that we're not who they say we are. It comes from a determined yet defiant mindset of "Well, I'll show you!"

The first two letters of *pridentity* stand for an identity forged out of our pride, aimed at proving, protecting, and preventing harm such as betrayal or rejection that we anticipate coming to us. It is rooted in ego defense mechanisms such as denial, projection, and overcompensation. These mechanisms help us cope with perceived threats to our self-image by creating a shield of pride and defiance.

This identity acts as a defensive barrier, rooted in reactive self-preservation rather than in embracing truth and purpose. It's an armor or shell used as a protective barrier shielding us from harm or having to be vulnerable. The concept of armor is addressed by Brené Brown, which I explained in chapter 1.

The impact of *pridentity* is that this constant need to prove ourselves and maintain a defensive posture can lead to significant emotional strain and stress. This can hinder emotional well-being, personal growth, and cause difficulties in forming genuine connections.

In professional settings, *pridentity* can impact workplace dynamics by fostering a competitive and sometimes hostile environment. Individuals may prioritize personal success over teamwork and collaboration. They may struggle with displaying vulnerability and the humility to admit mistakes. While *pridentity* may drive individuals to achieve professional success, it can also lead to burnout and dissatisfaction if achievements are solely pursued for external validation rather than intrinsic motivation.

Imagine who you would truly be without the need to prove to others that you should not be underestimated or underappreciated. Who would you become if you didn't feel the urge to prove, protect, or defend yourself? If your identity was shaped solely by the purity of your life purpose and who destiny created you to be, what would you be like? The time has come for you to discover your true self.

Healing the False Self Through Intentional Action

The problem that *labeliedentity* and *pridentity* present is that they are based on old narratives that diminish our power and agency. However, there is a better way that allows us to reclaim that agency. By crafting new, empowering stories that serve us, and by rewriting those stories through intentional action, we can transform our identities.

I opened this chapter by sharing how, due to my experiences as an asthmatic child, I saw myself as weak, sickly, and non-athletic. This was a *labeliedentity* that I accepted. However, the intentional actions of running regularly, surrounding myself with other runners, and immersing myself in running content helped me to dismantle the old identity. I began to see myself as a runner who was determined, resilient, and strong. A new script was written.

Discovering Your Real Identity Through Being Bold, Audacious, Courageous

As an intellectual, I must admit that sometimes I wish that deep change could happen simply through reading and studying. While I enjoy immersing myself in reading, reflecting, and theorizing, I realize that lasting change only materializes through taking action. Intentional action serves as the catalyst for the transformative journey that leads us to discover our true selves. The people who experience rapid and enduring change have a bias towards action. *Labeliedentity* and *pridentity* are like masks we wear in an effort to protect ourselves, but they ultimately prevent us from understanding who we truly are. Our real identity is pure and unencumbered by fears and doubts. To reestablish a connection with this authentic self, we need to actively engage in self-discovery—a quest to unveil our true essence and shed the facades we have constructed over time.

This adventure demands courage as we confront the aspects of ourselves that we've avoided facing. With each brave step forward, we cast off the chains of doubt and fear, embracing our ability to be Bold, Audacious, and Courageous! You may have forgotten the free-spirited, brilliant, unstoppable little girl you were before external forces restrained you. However, you cannot keep a good woman down for long—the true you is BAC! She is powerful.

Let's now explore how we can proactively discover our true selves through the intentional actions of being Bold Audacious, and Courageous.

BOLD

Throughout each chapter, we've used the acronym BOLD in the "bold actions" section to symbolize the act of breaking out of limits daringly. Boldness is a defining attribute of our essence. As bold women, we dare to reject all limits placed on us, especially those we impose on ourselves. We shatter those chains because we are fueled by the formidable force of our values, purpose, and mission, empowering us to break free from the shackles of fear that bind and limit us.

Key Characteristics of Boldness:

- Rejecting limits that are either self-imposed or externally imposed.
- Taking the risk of stepping outside of our comfort zones.
- Facing challenging situations with the confidence that we have what it takes, even if we have yet to acquire the necessary skills or knowledge. We trust in our ability to figure it out.

Values That Help You Tap into Boldness

The desire to contribute, develop, and grow.

How It Feels to Be Bold

Liberating and empowering. You feel as if you have agency because you have decided to own your power and be in control.

Metaphor for Boldness

Breaking free from chains.

Example of Bold Action

I used to see myself solely as a writer, using the power of words to make an impact. This self-perception gave me an excuse to hide behind a computer screen or a sheet of paper, shrinking back from vocal participation in meetings at work. My executive coach challenged me to level up my speaking skills. I proudly told her,

"I will just write; I don't have to speak." She then pointed out that the professional growth and impact I sought would be severely limited if I shied away from speaking. I had labeled myself as "not a speaker" to avoid taking risks. You see, speaking required me to show my face, stand on a stage, and look my audience in the eye. I didn't want to be rejected, but in order to grow I realized I had to first reject the limits I placed on myself. Why couldn't I be both a writer and a speaker? After all, great content, which I already had as a writer, is the foundation of powerful speaking.

Once I started speaking in meetings, on podcasts, YouTube, and even on stages, everything changed. I felt liberated, to become more influential and impactful. This bold action catalyzed both my professional and personal growth.

My journey reminds me of Neo from the 1999 movie "The Matrix," who lived in a simulated reality where his extraordinary powers were subdued. After choosing to take the red pill offered by his mentor Morpheus, Neo awakened to his true self and the power within him. This decisive action opened up a whole new world, allowing him to break free from the mental and physical chains that kept him in ignorance. I witness the same transformation in my clients time and again. When they take bold action and reject self-imposed or external limits, they become liberated and experience accelerated growth and professional transformation. What about you? Will you dare to be bold and break free from your chains. It's your time to activate the extraordinary power within you.

How to Be Bold

Identify an action that could enhance your professional development, yet you've hesitated to take due to it being outside your comfort zone. This action can involve being the first to voice your opinion in a meeting, engaging in a networking event, making a sales call, or delivering a speech on stage. Courageously take this step and record in your journal how it stretched you. Reflect on the impact this action had on both yourself and those around you.

Audacious

Being audacious is an important characteristic because it signifies a woman who is daring. There is a bigness about her that defies the odds. She defies being silenced. She defies adversity. She defies conformity. She shakes up the status quo and refuses to shrink, hide, or allow herself to be held back. She is a rebel with a cause, and that cause is good. She sets a new standard and is prepared to start some good trouble.

Key Characteristics of Being Audacious:

- Playing big by setting Big Hairy Audacious Goals and relentlessly pursuing them.

- Daring to step up and lead while being guided by a deep inner knowing that you are making the right move, even if it seems out of the box.

- Disregarding conventional expectations and processes because your proposal has the potential to yield exponential results.

Values That Help You Tap into Audaciousness
Adventure and experimentation.

How It Feels to Be Audacious
Exhilarating and exciting. The thrill of blowing past obstacles, crushing boundaries, and defying expectations is incredibly energizing and invigorating. It is like breathing new life into decaying bones.

Metaphor for Audacity

Skydiving, jumping out of the plane.

Example of Audacious Action

I once worked in a multi-national organization that was over 60% diverse. However, at the most senior levels, the diversity numbers were below 30%. I decided it was time to conduct a diversity training session on unconscious bias and develop a comprehensive plan to raise awareness of bias in the decision-making process for promotions. In this role, I was not part of the executive team, and most of the time, I was not even included in the discussions regarding top promotion decisions. As a result, my actions could have been perceived as overstepping boundaries. I also knew it would be disruptive to the organization's leaders because they believed they were doing well with such high overall diversity numbers. This was before 2020, when unconscious bias training was not yet popular or considered cool (although it is currently out of trend again as I write this in 2024, highlighting the performative and fickle nature of many organizations' commitment to creating equitable and inclusive cultures). Nevertheless, I moved forward because I deemed it worthwhile to face backlash if it meant disrupting a system that unconsciously limited opportunities for more diverse talent, which I knew would also ultimately have a negative impact on the business. I wasn't sure if my proposal would be accepted, but I decided to approach the entire process as an experiment in learning how to influence, and what a wild, adventurous ride it was. I managed to gain alignment from a few executives and the HR leader before conducting the training. So, when I faced opposition from the most senior leader in the room, I was prepared. Let me correct that—WE were prepared. I had backup. I successfully delivered three hours of training within a tight promotion meeting schedule, which was a significant achievement. The training had a small immediate impact on the decisions made in that meeting. However, weeks later, a leadership faux pas occurred, negatively affecting how leaders were perceived throughout the organization. Guess who was called upon and given permission to fully implement the DEI strategy and training proposed? If I hadn't been audacious enough to go against the grain, our organization might have missed an opportunity to transform its culture, which had positive implications for years to come.

How to Be Audacious

Identify an action that is aligned with the values and goals of your organization but could be perceived as shaking up the status quo. Discuss this action with your mentors, sponsors, and other leaders to seek their advice and support. This step is crucial because you want to avoid committing career suicide. Once your board of advisors is aligned, dare to lead by taking action. What happened? What insights did you gain?

Courageous

If bold and audacious feel like a tall order, courage is just what you need as you begin to embrace your true self. You can exhale a sigh of relief, though, because courage does not require you to be a superheroine. It does not mean the absence of fear; it means acknowledging fear and taking action despite it. Dear one, you don't have to feel ashamed because you experience fear. Instead, you can be relieved as you understand that fear comes with being a beginner, but confidence comes through attaining mastery. As you allow your actions to guide you through the advanced stages of development, fear naturally falls away. You don't have to force it or fight it; eventually, your actions deliver you from fear. Give yourself permission to be a beginner. By embracing the journey of being a beginner and mustering the courage to confront challenges head-on, you unlock the transformative power within to overcome fear and achieve remarkable growth.

True courage is not even possible without facing fear; however, it is the power to withstand and persevere through it all while you put one foot in front of the other, actively moving forward. When you have courage, you no longer avoid, but confront. You face obstacles; you do not flee from them. You tap into mental strength so you can keep moving ahead. Every courageous action you take proves that you are truly powerful and loosens the grip of fear in your life. These small millimeter shifts eventually lead to meteoric results.

Key Characteristics of Courage:

- Moving forward despite feeling fear.

- Opening the heart to new possibilities even when a positive outcome seems unlikely.

- Taking steps that bring steady change incrementally over time.

- Practicing stepping into one's power, like a toddler learning to walk; a person may fall, but they keep getting back up again.

Values That Help You Tap into Courage

Faith, hope, and discipline build the spirit and character to keep going even when there is no evidence that a positive outcome will happen.

How It Feels to Be Courageous

Hopeful and optimistic, even if uncertainty and instability lurk. While fear is present, determination fuels action, allowing you to push through negative feelings. This is where your vulnerabilities meet your power, and with each action, you grow into mastery because consistent actions improve your capabilities.

Metaphor for Courage

A baby learning to walk.

Example of Courageous Action

There were so many times when I was afraid to do something because of a fear of criticism, rejection, or failure. The examples ranged from having a difficult conversation with a colleague, asking for a raise, applying for a new job, or leading a new project I had no prior experience in. In the beginning, it felt scary because there was no guarantee of success, but when I pushed past that fear and took action anyway, I never lost, and neither will you. You will either win or you will learn a valuable lesson.

How to Be Courageous

Identify an action that you have not taken because you were afraid. Now, rise up, act, and keep going; never quit. If you fall or make a mistake, just get back up again. Focus on taking small, steady steps, and you will eventually reach your destination.

***

To embrace all that it means to be a BAC woman, it is essential that we nourish the mind to give it the strength needed to make it through. We feed our mind so that we can free it. Feeding the mind is done by consuming material that nourishes it rather than drains it.

What nourishes your mind and supplies it with the strength needed for tough situations? For me, it is reading spiritual texts like the Bible, inspirational quotes or books, listening to uplifting music, hearing someone else's life story of overcoming adversity, and watching certain movies or documentaries that give me hope. What drains my mind are negative people, certain types of social media, and media in general. When we know what we need to do to feed our minds and actually do it, we will have much of what we require to endure.

Once you receive strength through consuming inspirational material, what is the next step toward becoming a BAC woman? You work out! This entails actively pursuing your goals. We will never know what we are capable of if we don't do the metaphorical workout of taking action. While we know that the first step in building muscle is nourishment, we also understand that the next step is to lift weights to develop the strong muscles we desire.

Here's the catch: working out alone will exhaust, deplete, and potentially injure us, while solely consuming without exercising will pack on the pounds. Therefore, our fitness plan must be well-rounded and comprehensive. It is about having the fuel needed for the battle, engaging in the work, resting, refueling, and then reengaging. This is the cycle.

Engaging in BAC behavior is a great way to kickstart our transformation process. Every time we need to reprogram how we see ourselves, we return to taking bold, audacious, and courageous action. However, it is crucial to not only reap the benefits of this occasional practice but also to turn it into a daily habit to sustain our transformation journey. To develop the mental and spiritual strength required for consistently tackling the challenges ahead, we must embrace the The 6A Spiritual Practice for Courageous Women. This practice is not a quick fix that brings instant transformation. Just as we commit to a health plan and adhere to it for physical well-being, this practice demands daily dedication. We can't eat well, rest, or exercise once and expect lifelong benefits, in the same way these habits must be nurtured on a daily basis. We must consistently engage in the practice in the diagram below to fuel us with the strength needed to take consistent courageous action that leads to personal transformation and enables us to attain and sustain success.

The 6A Spiritual Practice for Courageous Women

The 6A Spiritual Practice for Courageous Women

1. Abiding

Abide means "to remain; continue; stay."[1] When we think of the word, we usually associate it with a physical location. However, as courageous women, we need a place to abide that extends far beyond the physical realm. This dwelling place must be so deeply ingrained within us that even in the face of turmoil and adversity, we remain steadfast and unyielding. This place is love.

In chapter 1, we discussed the importance of bringing in the love advocate as a strategy to quiet the inner critic. Now I invite you to embrace meditating on love as a daily spiritual practice that grounds, strengthens, heals, and serves as your ultimate source. Through the consistent practice of remaining, continuing, and staying in love, fear will lose its grip on you. Then, you will have the foundation from which to catapult yourself to extraordinary heights because you abide in love that's unconditional and un-shakable. The outcomes of your endeavors may vary, but the love you have for yourself is always constant and never in question.

Once you have this basis of love as the security on which you stand, you will experience a newfound sense of freedom because you've given yourself permission to pursue anything you desire, knowing that your self-love is not contingent upon your performance or achievements.

One of my favorite illustrations of this kind of love comes from an interview[2] basketball legend Kobe Bryant had with Lewis Howes, where Kobe recounts the story of complaining to his dad about how bad he'd played. Young Kobe, much to his dismay, did not score a single point in basketball games for the entire summer league with his peers. Overwhelmed by what he perceived as a personal failure, he cried and relayed what happened to his father.

In response, his dad lovingly said to him, "Whether you score zero or you score sixty points, I'm gonna love you no matter what."

It was at this point that Kobe said everything changed for him, because the love of the most important figure in his life would not be in question no matter how he performed. This is the power of unconditional love. When you give it to yourself as a foundation, you can use it as a springboard to accomplish anything. Maybe you didn't have a parent who expressed this type of unconditional love for you, but you can gift yourself with this nurturing and secure energy from this day forward. You can treat the child within you with kindness, compassion, and patience as you pursue your goals. It's a precious gift that you must consistently give yourself. That's why it's called a practice—something you engage in daily that has the incredible power to transform you forever if you wholeheartedly commit to it.

How do you practice abiding in love? Create space, even for just two minutes, to think about or write down the energy of love and direct it to yourself. For an entire year and a half, I listened to a love meditation on the Insight Timer app, and this practice completely changed me. You can search for love meditations on YouTube or your favorite meditation app. I've already referred to my love meditation[3] on YouTube. You can listen to it daily to help center yourself in love. I know I said I did this for eighteen months to rewire my brain, but you'd be surprised by the internal freedom you'll experience after just thirty days of consistently doing this.

Once you complete the meditation, wrap up this first step by writing down at least three to five things you love about yourself.

Here are my examples:

- Kisha, I love you because you have a curious mind.
- Kisha, I love you because you keep showing up, even when it's hard.

- Kisha, I love how you delight in ocean waves and white sandy beaches.

- Kisha, I love how you laugh.

- Kisha, I love how you care about your clients.

2. Awareness

Now that you've given yourself love as the foundation for being the bold woman you already are, the next step is cultivating simple awareness. This is the spiritual practice of recognizing the brilliant mystery of who you are by acknowledging your unique talents. It also entails noticing the moments of magnificence that unfold in your daily life.

Awareness of Your Strengths

List your strengths or talents below. You can write as many or as few as you want. My examples are:

- I'm innovative, always bringing out-of-the-box ideas to the work I do.

- I'm intuitive, able to activate my own inner wisdom to make decisions I can be confident in.

- I'm an intellectual; I like to analyze and challenge standard ways of thinking.

If you've done strengths-based assessments like the Fascinate Test®, these can serve as valuable resources for you to gain an understanding of some of your innate strengths and provide a starting point for this practice. As you engage in this awareness practice daily, you will gradually begin to name other strengths that you were previously unaware of. This presents yet another opportunity to discover more of the hidden treasures that reside within you.

Note that in the second half of this book, you'll be asked to conduct an informal 360-degree assessment where you will gather feedback from your colleagues regarding your core strengths. However, I intentionally included this activity at this stage to encourage you to learn to validate yourself daily. Many times, we find ourselves waiting for others to recognize and reward our strengths, only to be left waiting in vain.

By cultivating self-encouragement, you free yourself from relying on external validation. Take the time to acknowledge and affirm your own strengths daily. It's a great way to build up your self-confidence. And if others end up noticing what you do well, then graciously thank them and accept it. This is the icing on the cake, but you already had the cake completely baked before they complimented you because you validated yourself first.

Awareness of Moments of Magnificence

In addition to being aware of and acknowledging your strengths, this step invites you to also notice all the gifts that come into your life on a daily basis, whether they come in the form of people or circumstances. Taking the time to acknowledge these tiny moments of magnificence allows you to slow down and reflect on the goodness in your life. By engaging in this practice, you can cultivate more joy and contentment in a practical way.

Write down one tiny moment of magnificence (aka goodness) that occurred in your life today. Here are some examples that happened to me today:

- As I ran an errand in my city, a woman stopped me to say how she loved my dress. I paused to make time to tell her the story of how I purchased the dress, and it was a beautiful exchange. This was a quick two minutes of connection and joy with a complete stranger.

- I bought kombucha at the supermarket, and the cashier asked me what it was for, so I explained to her how I needed it to help with digestion, and she lit up when I spoke to her in Spanish. We ended up having a five-minute conversation where she told me about her family, where she was from, and what she liked to cook.

- Upon arriving at this market, I received the tiny miracle of getting the last parking spot close to the entrance on a busy Sunday.

Business Case Unleashed

Why companies should encourage their employees to become Bold, Audacious, and Courageous (risk taking and change agility).

By nurturing a culture that values courage and risk-taking, your company will cultivate a workforce that is more dynamic and forward-thinking. This leads to greater innovation, improved problem-solving, and a higher likelihood of achieving breakthrough results that add to the bottom line. Employees who feel liberated to be their authentic Bold, Audacious, Courageous selves will be unafraid to challenge the status quo and are positioned to drive transformation within the organization. This proactive stance can lead to a competitive advantage, as the company becomes better equipped to adapt to change and even lead it.

3. Appreciation

This is expressing gratitude for the goodness and gifts in your life. Once you're aware of and acknowledge these gifts, now is the time to appreciate them. Gratitude not only multiplies our happiness but also multiplies the gifts we experience.

This is a simple exercise: Write down three things you're grateful for by starting each sentence with "I'm grateful for . . ."

4. Affirmation

Now it's time to use your voice to verbally declare the ways in which you're awesome. These are more than just your strengths that we already called out in the awareness step; they include the qualities and characteristics that are part of your identity. Verbalizing your true identity through affirmations has a powerful impact because it activates different parts of our brain compared to just thinking. One study[4] published in the journal *Social Cognitive and Affective Neuroscience* used MRI to show that practicing self-affirmation activates the brain's reward centers, which may give us a happiness boost. Who wouldn't want a happiness boost?

You may be wondering: What will we use as the basis of our positive affirmations? In chapter 2, the inner DIVA, who is your inner coach, provided you with a list of qualities showing who you really are. Start with that list. Through this visualization, you've already begun the process of unveiling your true self. As you work to detach, shed, and discard the false self, you will increasingly connect with the real you. Here are a few additional qualities that I believe will resonate with you, even if only at a subconscious level:

- I am strong.
- I am lovely.
- I am great.
- I am powerful.
- I am mighty.

- I am victorious.

- I am glorious.

- I am resilient.

- I am talented.

- I am brilliant.

- I am gifted.

- I am wise.

- I am perfect just as I am.

- I am a walking miracle.

- I have what it takes.

- I am bold.

- I am audacious.

- I am courageous.

Feel free to personalize this list by adding any other phrases that resonate with you. These affirmations will gradually drown out the voice of the inner critic as you practice replaying them verbally and mentally over time. I personally conducted this experiment over an eighteen-month period when my inner critic was at an all-time high due to some challenging life circumstances. This practice helped me rewire my brain and supported me through that time. I'm confident that committing to this process has the potential to transform your life as well.

5. Action (BOLD)

This is where the rubber meets the road. All the affirmations in the world won't help you if you're not stepping up and taking courageous action. People don't make this connection often, but *taking action is spiritual*. This is because action demonstrates the depth of your faith. When you do something, it's never guaranteed that you will get the result you want. However, you still step out in faith to act, trusting that the outcome will be manifested even if it takes a while. It is here that the ethereal meets the earthly, where your beliefs are brought to life through your deeds.

You are positioned to win, so now is the time to take aligned action. Do the things you've always wanted to, whether it's making more sales calls, applying for that job, or approaching that mentor or potential sponsor. Author Jia Jiang did an inspiring hundred-day experiment where he set out to make some bold requests of people where he could encounter rejection on a daily basis. This was his way of doing something courageous every day. As a result of this experiment, he developed iron-steel confidence and resilience and had some life-changing experiences. His book *Rejection Proof: How I Beat Fear and Became Invincible Through 100 Days of Rejection*[5] is an inspiring model for staying in action by committing to one brave act each day to build up your courage. Earlier in this chapter, we asserted that fear is defeated and wiped out by the forced repetition of courage, Jia Jiang's experiment proved this truth.

Now it's your turn. Write down one action you took today that required you to use your courage muscle. This action must be something that required you to step out of your comfort zone—perhaps something you said, tried, or took a giant leap of faith to do.

Here's an example from when I was in the corporate world: I scheduled time with the chief human resources officer (CHRO), my one-over-one boss, to discuss my desire to apply for a higher-level role in the organization and ask for her support. You know what happened next? She gave it to me!

6. Applause

This is the concluding step in this spiritual process. I've come to the sad realization that we live in a world where we are vastly undercelebrated. Over the years, I notice that when I give my clients this simple exercise to celebrate themselves, it is often difficult for them to get started. It is such a foreign concept that they feel as if they won't have something to celebrate daily.

What about you? Do you think it will be hard to find something to celebrate about yourself each day for an extended period of time? If you're like me, it may seem that there is a never-ending list of self-improvement activities to engage in. Yet, we never look in the rearview mirror to see just how far we've come. The good news is you can change this situation today. When you applaud yourself first, everyone else applauding for you is a nice bonus but not necessary to feel good about yourself. Be your own hype woman. Celebrate yourself for all your efforts, not just the big ones. Let go of any attachment to the outcome. Focus on the fact that character is being shaped in you and will develop you. Know that you are investing in growing a healthy level of self-esteem. Whatever happens next, you've already won because you honored yourself and followed through.

Write down three things that you applaud or celebrate yourself for doing today. Here are some examples for me:

- Kisha, I applaud you for writing an entire chapter of your book in four hours today.

- Kisha, I applaud you for apologizing to your mom when you snapped at her.

- Kisha, I applaud you for not looking at social media or checking your phone before meditating this morning.

This Spiritual Practice Makes You Self Assured

The 6A Spiritual Practice for Courageous Women is character forming and builds authentic confidence that matures into self-assurance over time. You already know that I find it really unhelpful and impractical to tell someone to "just be more confident". This is why I love this spiritual practice—because it is a practical way to cultivate internal assurance.

When you regularly commit to this practice, you develop internal tenacity that allows you to take consistent, courageous action daily. These actions help you discover a new identity—your true self. Don't forget—every action you take, as author James Clear says, is a vote for the type of person you wish to be. Over time, you're building up evidence of this new identity.[6] In other words, as your actions accumulate, the shell of your false self begins to crumble, revealing ever increasing evidence of who you really are.

Self-assurance is the result of authentic confidence maturing over time. It's a deep-rooted knowing that you have what it takes, earned through consistent action. This allows you to develop competence and achieve results. It's an inner strength that doesn't need to prove, protect, or defend itself, as nothing, and no one, can shake how you see yourself. It is every DIVA's goal to attain self-assurance.

Warning on Taking Courageous Action

I would be remiss not to warn you that there will be instances when you step up to take BOLD Actions and the outcome won't be what you hoped for. I've experienced this many times myself. You can look at it as a failure, or you can look at it as part of the growth process. It's important that we reframe the outcome in a way that will motivate us to keep going until we find the approach that works for us.

Personally, I've found that connecting the outcome to a value that helps me cultivate resilience is best. Some people will reframe it as learning. Others may reframe it as an adventure where they can experiment until they find the answer. Regardless of the approach you adopt, it's vital not to use it as an opportunity to shame yourself or interpret it as a reflection of your inherent inadequacy.

When your BOLD Actions result in less-than-desirable outcomes (at least in the short term), look at these events as character-building opportunities that will help you grow, build your courage muscle, and ignite a fire within you to keep going until you find a way that works. You're evolving into an unstoppable woman who refuses to be deterred. While you remain open to constructive feedback, you will not allow your voice to be silenced. You will rise up and embrace every obstacle you face as a stepping stone on your journey toward success!

Unleashing the Next Chapter

Imagine the empowering sensation of entering your workplace with unshakable confidence, adeptly navigating office politics with finesse, and no longer being blindsided by it. In the upcoming chapter, you will master The DIVA Method®, my proprietary approach designed to propel you to new career heights. This method will equip you to deliver outstanding results, cultivate your professional brand, and gain the visibility you need to achieve your loftiest career aspirations. As you delve into the next chapter, you are stepping into the winner's circle, surrounded by a formidable support network ready to shield you from any professional land mines you may encounter.

BOLD Actions to Evoke Your Transformation

1. *__Intersectional reflection question__*: Have you constructed either or both of the false selves—*labeliedentity* or *pridentity*—to cope with an intersectional factor such as your culture, ethnicity, disability, mental health status, native language, etc.? If so, journal how it has affected your ability to step into your true self.

2. Is there any part of the 6A Spiritual Practice for Courageous Women that you already engage in? Which ones have you never done?

3. Commit to practicing at least one part of the spiritual practice for thirty days, and journal how it is impacting you. Perhaps you will feel inspired to go all-in on your transformation by adding a new component monthly to build up to all six over six months. Do this, and in six months, you will be such a courageous woman that you will become barely recognizable to yourself!

To wrap up the first half of this book, I am throwing in some additional exercises for those of you committed to going all in on your transformation. They are optional.

Optional Bonus BOLD Actions

✓ What if taking courageous action blows up in your face? How would you respond based on the insights shared in this chapter? Have you experienced this before? If so, how did you handle it, and what will you do differently now?

✓ The time has come for you to file for a divorce from self-doubt and fear. Write a breakup letter explaining the reason for the filing.

✓ Today is your wedding day, where you and the new *BAC you* will become one forever. Write your marriage vows declaring your commitment to the Bold, Audacious, Courageous you!

PART TWO

PART TWO

Your Power Unleashed®—Savvy Workplace Strategies

PART TWO

PART TWO

PART TWO

CHAPTER SIX

The DIVA Method® — Your Career GPS (Get Promoted Strategy)

Success is 20 percent skills and 80 percent strategy.
—Jim Rohn

"I don't know what happened in the last six months, but prior to this year, I'd never heard of this woman. Now, seemingly out of the blue, I can't escape hearing about what an incredible rock star she is and all the amazing work she's been doing for this organization. It's as if her name is everywhere I turn. She's involved in key initiatives. Leaders approach me to sing her praises during site visits. I've received emails highlighting her impact. And just last week, I saw her deliver a strong presentation at the midyear operations review. What's the story? Where has she been all this time, and why am I only now discovering her?"

These were the words of our curious senior vice president (SVP) during the department's promotion review meeting as he looked at me, waiting for answers.

I smiled a bit, chuckling internally as I thought, *Yes, our strategy worked!* Guadalupe (Lupe) Mendoza was finally getting all the visibility and credit for her hard work, something she had never received in the past. As the human resources leader, I would not let another top-performing woman slip through the cracks. I remembered how I'd lost the battle to secure a high-potential associate a year ago: Aaliyah was an excellent employee whose manager thought she was ready to advance to the next level, but he and I were both blindsided when we got to the meeting and another leader who'd managed her years before was adamant that she was not ready for a career jump. She wasn't promoted despite a full year of strong performance because she didn't have enough sponsors for her at the decision-making table to compensate for that one very vocal detractor. I got heartburn every time I thought about what a loss this was, and I vowed that I would never let that happen again as long as I had the power to influence things. This time, I ensured that the SVP and a carefully selected group of influential decision-makers would continue hearing about Lupe's accomplishments, thanks to myself and a few of her other mentors. None of this was coincidental; it was all part of a carefully orchestrated plan.

Rewind to six months before, when I was conducting a site visit to one of our locations in Houston. During a local Hispanic employee resource group (ERG) event, a leader approached me and said, "I heard you were going to be here, and I know the promotion discussions are approaching. The folks at your HQ office have no idea what a rock star Lupe is, but this woman has the trajectory to become CFO of one of our tier-two businesses. She's the smartest financial analyst that I've seen come through our business in a long time, but I'm concerned that the right people aren't aware of her abilities. Kisha, I need you to relay this message to the HQ decision-makers."

This wasn't the first time I'd encountered this type of conversation. Aaliyah had also had supporters in the business who knew her excellent track record, but I discovered too late that they lacked the organizational clout to secure her promotion. Therefore, as soon as I returned to my office in Boston, I sat down and mapped out a promotion plan for Lupe. The first thing I did was have a conversation with her to gauge her mindset. Lupe echoed the same sentiments that Aaliyah had expressed, stating that she was not a political person and asserting that her hard work and impressive track record would speak for themselves. She mistakenly believed that her results alone would get her promoted. This was the myth of meritocracy that she had bought into, and I had to dispel her tragic naivete.

"Listen, Lupe," I said firmly, "that's not how it works. Hard work is just a small part of the equation to get ahead, but it's not a concrete strategy. You also need to ensure that you have a strong brand. Decision-makers need to know who you are, and you must garner visibility, sponsorship, and access."

The first step in my plan was to give her the insider secrets that would help her overcome the beliefs hindering her success. This conversation played a pivotal role in launching Lupe's journey of self-improvement. I worked with her to develop her organizational savvy by providing insights that would enable her to navigate the company while remaining true to herself. It was crucial for her to understand that being strategic about her career did not equate to being inauthentic or engaging in icky political tactics. She needed to recognize that there were specific steps she could take that would put her in the driver's seat of her professional journey. Once Lupe shifted her mindset and implemented a strategic approach with the guidance of her mentors, she began to receive the promotions she rightfully deserved. This, in turn, opened doors to many new opportunities for her.

Lupe's story is a powerful lesson—a reminder that being organizationally savvy and strategic is not about engaging in negative politics. It's about understanding the dynamics of the workplace, cultivating relationships, managing stakeholders, and making strategic decisions that align with your career goals. By embracing a new mindset and adopting this approach, just like Lupe, you can achieve remarkable results in your profession by taking charge of your career and becoming the designer of your own success.

Over the next few chapters, I will guide you in developing the same savvy skills that Lupe attained, so you're not another well-deserving professional woman overlooked for the opportunities she truly deserves.

Organizationally Savvy

Let's delve into the distinction between being political and being savvy. We can all agree that in order to thrive in the corporate world, it's crucial to develop interpersonal skills that assist us in navigating complex work structures. The question then arises: How do we accomplish that? As a coach, I recognize that the language we use can significantly impact our motivation to act and achieve our desired outcomes.

Many individuals aspire to succeed in their professional lives; however, if they believe that being political is a prerequisite for success, they may become disengaged. This is because the term political carries a negative connotation, evoking images of being manipulative, dishonest, power hungry, slick, toxic, and self-centered—individuals who prioritize personal gain over the well-being of others. Naturally, no one wishes to be perceived as political when this is the prevailing image associated with it.

How do we convey the importance of acquiring the skills to successfully navigate complex organizational structures as women who desire to advance in their careers *sans* the toxicity? The answer lies in the word *savvy*.

A savvy woman knows the importance of understanding her work environment, including power dynamics and relationships among different stakeholders. It's not solely about gaining an understanding of these relationship dynamics but also being adept at influencing and persuading others to support her ideas to achieve favorable outcomes. Instead of shying away from this challenge, she recognizes the need to build relationships across the organization to accomplish her goals while carefully managing how others perceive her.

A savvy woman who possesses interpersonal, influencing, and relational skills can effortlessly navigate through political structures and seize opportunities that enhance her career, benefit her team, and position the organization for success. Mastering these skills is not easy, and some might argue that it's even more challenging than excelling in the technical aspects of your job. If we avoid developing these skills simply because we mistakenly associate them with toxicity and politics, we won't excel in the workplace. It's not about being a jerk; it's about being wise.

When we embrace savviness over naivete from a place of purpose, we not only maximize our own potential at work but also contribute in meaningful ways to the company that employs us and utilize our unique talents in the service of others. This is what a DIVA who unleashes her power does. A DIVA is a savvy woman who takes charge of her career by delivering results; building a strong image (aka brand); garnering visibility with the right decision-makers; and proactively establishing her advisory board with coaches, mentors, and sponsors who will help her accelerate her career.

I've witnessed the effectiveness of this time-tested, four-step DIVA Method throughout my decades-long experience coaching employees in more than fifty countries globally. From Fortune 500 companies to law firms to midsize and small organizations, these strategies work. Initially I employed them during my tenure in human resources at General Electric, advising early, midcareer, and senior leaders on how to advance professionally. I continue to utilize these principles in my consulting work with numerous organizations across multiple industries globally. I share this background because I want you to understand that regardless of where you work, these principles hold true. Many of us didn't grow up in households with parents who were corporate executives; I certainly didn't. We were told that hard work alone would be sufficient. However, we now know that hard work without a holistic plan for advancement is an illusion.

To succeed you must have a vision of your professional goals, put in the necessary work, get to know the decision-makers, and develop organizational savvy to successfully navigate the political landscape in the workplace. The DIVA Method® provides a way to achieve just that. My hope is that, after reading this chapter, you will no longer be naive about what it takes to get ahead but rather become a savvy DIVA who takes charge of her career!

The DIVA Method®

Step 1: Deliver Results

If you're from a middle-class, blue-collar, or immigrant family (which applies to the majority of us!), chances are that this strategy has been thoroughly ingrained in you: work hard and deliver results. This is undeniably true. If you're not delivering in your role and meeting expectations, this book will not save you. Nothing will. The rest of this method is predicated on your doing the work on time and with excellence. This includes doing what you say you're going to do, doing it consistently, and having a high say/do ratio.

Reliability: High Say/Do Ratio

The say/do ratio is a measure of someone's reliability that compares what they say they will do with the degree to which they actually follow through. This is about keeping one's commitments and consistently delivering high-quality work on time. If you're viewed as someone who consistently delivers on their commitments, stakeholders will view you as reliable and trustworthy, paving the way for increased opportunities to come your way.

Knowing Your Organization's Unwritten Rules of Success

To consistently meet the expectations of your company, it's crucial to know what the measure of success is. What behaviors do you need to display to be viewed as someone with the potential to succeed in that organization? If you're new to a firm, it will take time to familiarize yourself with the culture and understand what it takes to get to the top. As a new employee, it's a good idea to seek out a longer-tenured person who will give you the insights you need in order to get ahead. Ask the HR team or your manager to provide you with a buddy to show you the ropes if they haven't already done so, and you can also ask members of the new team you're on to share insights. Even if you've been with an organization for some time, each team or department has a distinct culture with unwritten rules. Therefore, learning the expectations from legacy members of the team is highly recommended.

Consistently delivering results via high-quality, on-time work and according to the expectations of the leader that you work for puts you in a great position to build a good reputation that will help you shape the narrative of what others are saying about you when you're not in the room. This off-the-record or unofficial reputation, if not managed proactively, can be absolutely devastating to one's career, especially since you may not be aware of what is being said about you behind closed doors.

I've sat in rooms with senior leaders where discussions veered off topic, focusing on aspects such as what women wore to work—bright colors, offbeat hairstyles, and short skirts—diverting attention from their competence and ability to perform their jobs effectively. Similarly, I've witnessed conversations about men with strong body odors, which negatively impacted their potential for advancement due to other people's reluctance to be around them.

Although it's impossible to know everything being said about you when you're not in the room, you can do two things: first, build relationships of trust with individuals at all levels; and second, actively seek feedback from them. This increases the likelihood of someone sharing information that may be in your blind spot. This is especially important for women and people of color because research[1] shows that women are more than 20 percent less likely than men to say their manager gave them critical feedback that helped them improve their performance.

Additionally, a survey[2] revealed that Black and Latinx employees were more likely to receive job performance feedback that was both negatively biased and not actionable. Nonactionable feedback, if you're wondering, usually revolves around personality traits and tends to be vague. For instance, instead of being provided with specific, actionable feedback such as "You often interrupt people in meetings," individuals may be told something general like "You're irritating."

In the first example, the recipient knows the specific behavior that needs to be addressed, which is interrupting others. When feedback fails to focus on specific behaviors, it's challenging for the recipient to take meaningful action to improve.

Considering these challenges in getting helpful feedback, ensure that you proactively ask for it. Since most people don't love giving feedback, make it easy for others to do so by remaining receptive, open, and curious during the conversation. Taking it a step further, you should follow up after the conversation to let them know which actions you've taken as a result of the feedback you received. This not only shows that you value feedback but also reassures the person providing it that their time was well spent. By demonstrating that you take feedback seriously, you encourage these individuals to continue sharing their insights and perspectives with you.

Another important thing within your control is consistently following through on your work. When you always deliver, it becomes difficult for others to dispute or question your capabilities. Although you may still face occasional challenges when managing your brand, doing this part well will make the process a lot easier.

Step 2: Image

Who is in charge of your reputation? Your reputation is another word for your brand. You don't have to be a brand expert or even a brand-focused person to have a brand. Everyone has one. The key question is whether you're purposefully shaping and managing your brand image or simply allowing it to unfold haphazardly. You have the choice to take control of building your brand, or you can allow it to develop by chance. The issue with the latter is that if it accidentally develops, the brand is happening to you rather than for you.

Celebrities understand that their personal brand plays a crucial role in their careers and can significantly impact their success. Let's talk about Beyoncé, for example. When you think about her, what comes to mind? For me, the words are powerful, fierce, stylish, beautiful, and artistically excellent.

Beyoncé and her management team have made a conscious effort to maintain control over her image. They ensure that her public appearances, social media presence, and interviews always align with her brand. This carefully curated image is so brilliant that, along with her outstanding work, it has inspired a fiercely loyal community of fans called the BeyHive.

We don't all have a management team like Beyoncé, but that doesn't mean we cannot be strategic and intentional about building, nurturing, and establishing a professional brand at work. Below are some simple steps that you can take to begin positioning your brand in your organization.

Activity to Assess Where Your Brand Is Now

The first step in building your brand is to assess where you are now versus where you want to be. To do so, follow these steps:

- Ask five to ten people to share five words that come to mind when they think of your strengths.

- Have them note one area of improvement that would enhance your effectiveness.

Suggest that they send their responses via email or text for efficiency. This exercise should only take a few minutes to complete. It's an effective strategy because it allows people to primarily focus on highlighting your strengths, which makes them more comfortable providing transparent feedback regarding your areas of development. Additionally, by requesting only one improvement area, they will be more inclined to tell you the area that's most significant to work on. Once you get this feedback, review it, assess the gap, and create a plan.

- Review the feedback: As you review the information you received, ask yourself a few questions: *What feedback resonated with me the most? Were there any common themes in the areas of strength and development? How can I leverage my strengths to accelerate my success professionally? How can I work on my areas of development?*

- Assess the gap: How do you want to be seen in the organization? Is there a gap between your current image and where you aspire to be? If there is a gap, what will you need to do to bridge it? Consider what it will take for you to get to the next level. What specific skill sets do you need to acquire or enhance? How do you need to be perceived within the organization to achieve your desired goals?

- Create a plan: Once you've completed the steps above, create a plan to develop the brand you desire.

When I did this exercise over a decade ago, the feedback I received was:

- Safe and welcoming: People thought I was approachable and that I created an environment of safety and nonjudgment—they would be comfortable telling me anything.

- Insightful: I was perceptive and saw things that others missed; I could translate the insights into tactical actions that people could use.

- Honest: Others could depend on me to tell the truth, which was quite an accomplishment since so many employees automatically didn't trust HR staff. They knew I would deliver the message in a clear and direct way. But at the same time, I was sensitive to their feelings.

- Open: I had strong opinions but always displayed a willingness to hear the other side.

- Solutions-oriented: People felt that whenever there was a challenge, I would think of innovative ways to solve the problem.

A common theme in the developmental feedback I received was that while I am generally an upbeat person, there are times when I become unhappy with something, and it's evident because I withdraw and become reclusive. In other words, I tend to shut people out, which contradicts the safe and welcoming environment I usually strive to create. This is not something I'm proud of, but as someone who leans toward introversion, it's important for me to actively work on managing this tendency so that it doesn't hinder my professional effectiveness. By being proactive and finding ways to prevent this derailer from being activated, I can take strides to manage its impact. Interestingly, I took a strengths-based assessment called the Fascinate Test®, and it had very similar findings about my areas of development. If you'd like to take this assessment, go to the resources section of this book for more details.

Business Case Unleashed

Why companies should help their employees implement The DIVA Method® (fulfillment and belonging).

When employees are equipped to master The DIVA Method®, they feel a sense of professional fulfillment and belonging because they have the resources necessary to achieve career success, including a supportive professional community. This yields significant benefits for the company in three ways:

1. Better Business Outcomes: It improves performance, which contributes directly to improved outcomes.

2. Increased Retention and Engagement: Having a strong internal network fosters a deep sense of belonging among employees, which is a powerful driver of employee retention and engagement. When employees feel valued, connected, and supported, they are more likely to stay committed to the organization.

3. Positive Work Environment: The conditions created by mastering The DIVA Method® allow employees to collaborate more effectively, share knowledge, and contribute to a positive work environment, which further drives business success.

How Do I Want to Be Seen?

As I reviewed my areas of strength, there were no real surprises. However, I decided that I wanted to be known as someone who used the skill set of coaching to facilitate cultural transformation within the organization. My goal was to model what being a great coach was and influence others to adopt a coach-like approach in their personal interactions. By doing so, I hoped to help build a high-performing learning culture, moving away from the prevailing command-and-control one that was present.

The second thing I wanted to be known for was being someone who helped foster an inclusive environment where people of all backgrounds could thrive. This was relevant to the organization I worked for because, at the time, we had a population that was 65 percent globally diverse.

These two issues were perfect because they represented areas I was passionate about and where I had competency. Equally important, however, was that they were aligned with the organization's needs. The best brand pillars to help you succeed at your company are those that are aligned with what the organization needs and areas you're authentically interested in.

As you can see from the exercise above, the brand that I developed was not accidental but intentional. I determined what I wanted to be known for and got to work implementing a plan to make it happen. I checked in with myself using a spreadsheet in the beginning to track and ensure that I was consistently doing things to support the image that I wanted to have. These things included coaching others, training managers on coaching skills, and conducting diversity, equity, and inclusion (DEI)–related sessions. Once you decide what you want to be known for, a key part of the strategy is coming up with a list of actions that you can take that will support your brand image.

I no longer work as a corporate employee, but to this day, there are still people I worked with in that organization who reach out to get coaching or ask me to do diversity-related projects in the companies they now work for. This is a result of all the brand work I did years ago. When you develop a strong brand, it will pay dividends for years to come.

Step 3: Visibility

Once you've established the foundations for delivering outstanding results and cultivating an intentional and authentic image, the next step is to gain visibility. It's pointless to be the greatest at what you do while being the best-kept secret in town. Even if you bring immense value, if the right people are unaware of your capabilities, you will not maximize the benefits of all your hard work. Visibility is key to executing the strategic plan that you created in the image-building phase of developing your brand.

Mindset plays a huge part in whether or not we will give ourselves permission to be visible, so it's imperative that we start here. Over the years, so many of my brilliant clients have hidden from the spotlight because of mental barriers. We shy away from visibility due to past experiences of feeling marginalized or for various reasons that make us feel unworthy. These experiences trigger self-doubt and fear. In chapter 4, we explored manifestations of fear, which examines the messages fear carries.

According to author Karla McLaren,[3] fear has hidden messages that she refers to as gifts. Take a moment to identify the gift that this fear of visibility might be offering you. Perhaps it's an invitation for personal growth and an opportunity to cultivate courage. By acknowledging and understanding the underlying message, you can work toward embracing visibility with a positive mindset. Whatever the message is, in moments when you feel vulnerable due to the fear of attention and visibility, practice graceful compassion toward your tender heart. Embrace the sacredness of your current situation and let it usher you into deeper healing. This healing process will address the inner wounds that have been exposed by your resistance to opening up and being seen, if you allow it. Invite your inner coach to be with you and guide you on this journey. Now, with courage, let's move on to the tactics.

Take the High-Visibility Project: Taking on a challenging, high-visibility project comes with inherent risks. If you don't perform well, everyone will know about it. However, if you excel, it can lead to career advancement opportunities because it demonstrates your capability to handle complex or important initiatives. When influential decision-makers become aware of a star in their midst, great things can happen.

Take the Tough Assignment: Similar to the high-visibility project, there are risks involved in taking on a challenging assignment. However, the potential benefits can greatly outweigh those risks. By accepting such a task, you have the opportunity to develop new skills and gain valuable experience that can open up future career opportunities for you. Moreover, successfully executing difficult assignments boosts your self-confidence and demonstrates to yourself and others that you're capable of overcoming challenges. As a result, leaders will have more confidence in your abilities because you stepped up and excelled in a demanding area. Sometimes, you have to take a bet on yourself first before others will take a bet on you!

Engage in Networking Proactively: Networking will help you build strategic relationships with people who can be key to your career success. I heard a leader emphasize how important it is to make a friend before you need one, and it truly struck a chord with me. People oftentimes wait until they're in a jam before reaching out for help. However, by proactively building alliances in advance, you can potentially provide a soft landing in a tough situation and make challenging circumstances more manageable. Additionally, having an expanded network can open doors to unforeseen opportunities that may propel your career at an accelerated pace.

Volunteer for Events and Committees: Engaging in volunteer work for events and committees, including roles in ERGs, can bring numerous benefits. However, it's important to ensure that you consistently perform well in your actual job and be mindful of avoiding burnout. Volunteering for committees provides a natural opportunity to establish relationships with colleagues with whom you might not typically interact. It serves as a way to organically expand your network within the organization, particularly if you're one of those people who hesitates to initiate meetings with individuals they don't know. Participating in these committees not only facilitates skill development but also exposes you to new opportunities for career advancement within the workplace.

Speak Up in Meetings: Sometimes enhancing your visibility, brand, and reputation within an organization doesn't require you to do the most. It can be as straightforward as making a strong and impactful impression during the meetings you already attend. Rather than shrinking back and hiding due to fear or merely adopting a passive presence, you can challenge yourself to speak up and share your valuable insights. Alternatively, you can ask thought-provoking questions that redirect the course of a conversation. Although it may require some preparation beforehand, if you approach each opportunity with dedication and enthusiasm, you might open up even more doors for yourself.

Develop Strong Relationships with Your Boss and Other Leaders: Your boss, ideally, should serve as your sponsor, and it's critical to effectively manage the dynamics with this person. However, there may be instances where improving a relationship with a challenging manager is not feasible. In such cases, it's advisable to strategize a transition away from reporting to them as soon as possible. This is why it's important to establish connections with other decision-makers in your area of the organization. By doing so, you avoid relying solely on one individual for your professional advancement. The relationship with your manager will have the most immediate and significant impact on your career trajectory in the short term. However, by nurturing these relationships with other decision-makers, you can enhance your long-term career success.

Teach Something That You're an Expert In: Via lunch-and-learn sessions, webinars, and so on, this unconventional approach can boost your visibility and establish you as a thought leader inside and outside your company. Teaching not only enhances your visibility and opens up potential advancement opportunities, but it can also bring you personal satisfaction as you utilize your skills to mentor and contribute to the success of others.

Step 4: Advisory Board

When Steven Reinemund, the former CEO of PepsiCo, was promoted to that role, he refused to take the position unless Indra Nooyi served as his second in command.[4] This fierce sponsorship played a role in her eventual promotion to president of PepsiCo. This is a great illustration of the power of mentorship and sponsorship, which can open doors for you that you cannot open for yourself. Indra Nooyi was already a high-performing, proven leader, and this allowed her to garner the support of an influential individual to her personal board of directors, which in turn propelled her career.

The last step of The DIVA Method® is to establish your personal board of directors, also known as your advisory board. This board comprises strategic key relationships that you develop or hire. These board members should have the ability to challenge and stretch you outside of your comfort zone and encourage you to make bold moves. They will serve as a sounding board, providing valuable advice, feedback, and diverse perspectives. Additionally, having powerful allies who have your back within your organization is crucial.

Some of the Roles That Should Be on Your Personal Board of Directors

Mentor: A mentor is someone with experience in your current situation who can offer valuable advice, knowledge, and insight to accelerate your learning and prevent pitfalls. For instance, a working mother who has successfully integrated her career aspirations and parenting commitments can be your mentor. This is especially beneficial if you are also learning how to navigate being a working mother. You can learn best practices from her.

Connector: A connector helps you expand your network. This is a person who enjoys connecting people to each other, whether it's a peer, a junior-level employee, or an executive.

Insightful Expert: An insightful expert could be a mentor or peer, but this person has deep knowledge in an area where you do not.

Coach: A coach supports you in effectively utilizing the rest of your board. They assist you in formulating strategies, gaining clarity, overcoming mental barriers such as fears and limiting beliefs, identifying blind spots and root causes, and holding you accountable for your actions. Consider the work of sports coaches, who transform good athletes into exceptional ones by helping them refine their techniques. Similarly executive career coaches can help you win professionally.

A skilled coach, who may be the one person on your board that you need to hire, doesn't necessarily require expertise in your specific field. They will, however, prioritize your goals and agenda and engage you in coaching conversations that help you identify and navigate hurdles that hinder your progress. These obstacles might be internal, tactical, or due to a lack of competence. The coach's role is to assist you in identifying and overcoming these obstacles, bridging the gap between where you are and where you want to be.

As a coach, I've supported numerous people in mastering skills such as managing difficult relationships, developing leadership or executive presence, delegating tasks effectively to their teams, enhancing confidence and assertiveness, having difficult conversations, setting boundaries, improving emotional intelligence, fine-tuning their influencing or communication skills, building stress resiliency, improving strategic thinking skills, and leveraging their network. There are a wide range of topics that can be covered in coaching. By collaborating with a coach, you can co-create a strategy tailored to your unique abilities and needs. If you find the right coach who can challenge you and hold a safe space for your growth, this resource can help you to significantly accelerate your career in remarkable ways.

A word of warning—just because someone has an Instagram or LinkedIn account and labels themselves as a coach doesn't mean they possess the necessary training and expertise to effectively assist you in overcoming the habits that are sabotaging your professional success. Although some may have industry-specific experience akin to that of a mentor, a well-trained coach will possess a repertoire of tools and strategies designed to help you achieve your desired outcomes rather than simply sharing their own success story. To ensure you engage with a reputable coach, it's advisable to seek someone who has obtained certification from an accredited coaching school recognized by the International Coaching Federation.

Sponsor: While mentors are habitually emphasized as essential for career advancement, there is an even more important and frequently overlooked relationship that can rapidly propel our careers: sponsorship. In the business world, it seems like every leadership expert stresses the role of mentors. While they are indeed important, as I've highlighted above, they are not the only people we need on our personal board of advisors. Many experts tend to overlook the even more potent asset of sponsorship, which, if utilized effectively, can rapidly propel our careers. In her book *Executive Presence: The Missing Link Between Merit and Success*, Sylvia Ann Hewlett argues that sponsors are more powerful than mentors because they have a greater vested interest in our progress.[5] I believe they are more invested because they have essentially become a co-brand with the person they support. As a result, the success achieved by the sponsored person reflects positively on the sponsor and their brand. No one wants to jump onto a sinking ship, but someone viewed as a rising star will attract numerous individuals who will want to associate their names (and brands) with theirs.

As illustrated by the story of Steven Reinemund's sponsorship of Indra Nooyi, sponsors possess the power, connections, and influence to utilize their social capital to get you promoted, secure plum assignments, and even provide protection as you navigate the learning curve. Without influence, a leader may not be able to serve as a sponsor because you need someone to open doors for you that you don't currently have access to. Sponsorship is about gaining access, and as an ambitious professional, having access is crucial for advancing your career. Women are more likely to be satisfied with their career progress when they have a sponsor because, as highlighted in the *Harvard Business Review* (*HBR*) article "Why Men Still Get More Promotions Than Women," "without sponsorship, a person is likely to be overlooked for promotion, regardless of his or her competence and performance."[6]

According to the article, there are multiple reasons why mentoring programs are much less effective for career advancement versus sponsorship, and I will highlight four of them below.

1. *Feedback focused instead of advocacy focused:* Mentoring programs prioritize the mentor providing advice or feedback to the mentee. Although this can be beneficial, it may become merely busywork if it fails to contribute to the mentee's promotion. In contrast, sponsors use their influence with other senior executives to advocate for their protégés to get promoted; this is the end game!

2. *Mentors may lack decision-making influence in the organization:* Mentoring programs typically assign nice, well-meaning leaders who are not high enough up in the company to help you advance. Middle managers, in particular, usually don't have enough clout to get you promoted to top positions, but they can be valuable if they have the decision-makers' ears. Sponsors are usually senior executives who have the authority to either hire you into a bigger role themselves or tell others to get it done.

3. *Chemistry match versus clout:* Mentors at times are selected in programs because they may have good chemistry with mentees. Sponsors are selected because they have power, influence, and authority. Let's leave chemistry matches to reality TV dating shows.

4. *Goodwill versus accountability:* Mentors are typically requested to help mentees based on goodwill, which means

it's optional for them to advocate for you even if they hold influential positions. Sponsors, in many sponsoring programs, are held accountable for achieving specific targets, and given the competitive nature of businesspeople, they are more incentivized to actively push to get their people promoted.

Challenge your organization to prioritize creating sponsorship opportunities rather than focusing solely on mentoring. One exception that can be made is if the mentors they assign to you can and are expected to fulfill a dual role as both mentor and sponsor. This way, you benefit from the advantages of both mentorship and sponsorship. Share this section of this book with your HR leader, as well as the *HBR* article referenced. I wish I had this information regarding the effectiveness of sponsorship years ago when I was busy designing mentoring programs as an HR professional.

Here's the bottom line: If you don't have a sponsor, you're missing a vital resource in your tool kit for achieving career success. It's as simple as that.

The advisory board step follows visibility in The DIVA Method® because visibility is crucial in capturing the attention of individuals who may potentially join your board. This is particularly important when it comes to finding a sponsor, as sponsors typically discover and approach you rather than the other way around. Therefore, it's essential to position yourself in a way that facilitates discovery through the visibility actions previously discussed.

How to Leverage Your Advisory Board

After teaching The DIVA Method® framework, one common question I receive from participants is: "How can I effectively leverage my personal board of directors once it's established?" The following are some best practices you can employ for effectively utilizing your board:

1. **Establish regular communication with your board members.** Schedule periodic meetings or check-ins with your advisory board. You can do so in person, by phone, or via videoconferencing. Consistent communication will strengthen your relationship with your board members and lead to mutual trust and respect. It also ensures that you receive timely advice, support, accountability, and updates on your brand reputation.

2. **Come prepared for each meeting with your advisory board by having a clear purpose and agenda.** This will ensure that the sessions are productive and efficient, allowing you to make the most of their valuable expertise and insights.

3. **If you take an action, follow up and report your progress.** Whenever someone takes time out of their calendar to meet with you, it's important to demonstrate that you value and appreciate their time by taking action in the areas agreed upon. When you circle back with them to share outcomes and insights related to the action you took, they will experience a level of fulfillment, knowing that they contributed to your professional development and personal transformation.

4. **Reverse mentoring offers the opportunity to reciprocate in the mentor-mentee relationship.** Although most mentors will not expect you to provide anything in return except following through on your commitments and taking your own development seriously, you can surprise them by reciprocating value in return. By learning what matters to your board, you can offer your support

and contribute to their goals through reverse mentoring. Some common ways in which I've seen more junior employees mentor senior-level executives include social media and digital communication, technological trends, diversity and inclusion from the perspective of someone in your demographic, emerging consumer trends, and innovative ideas that come from having a fresh perspective.

The DIVA Method® is a career momentum builder that encompasses four phases, each building upon the progress of the previous one. This momentum has enough energy to help you smash through any professional barrier that gets in your way. Once that career train gets going, it will pick up speed and help you blast your career to new heights. Creating momentum does require an initial investment of effort and work, and starting to build that initial traction is the most challenging part. Yet, with every action you take and every measure of success attained, it breeds more opportunities and increases confidence, which, in turn, attracts more success. Do the work now to get that train started, and over time, you will reap the rewards of investing in yourself.

Take The DIVA Method® Get Promoted Savvy Quiz

Now that you are well versed in all the steps of The DIVA Method®, it's time to assess your likelihood of being promoted or advancing professionally in your current organization. Visit my website at https://www.yourpowerunleashed.org/bookresources to take the Get Promoted Savvy quiz. Once you complete the quiz, if you identify any gaps in your career advancement strategy, develop a solid plan based on everything you learned in this chapter to fill in those gaps and overcome any obstacles that may be holding you back.

Paying It Forward

Here are some final thoughts for this chapter: As DIVAs, we strongly believe in the power of paying it forward. Just as others have invested in us, it's important for us to take the time to invest and give back by being on someone else's board. Regardless of where you are in your career, there is always someone who can benefit from your knowledge through mentoring, imparting your expertise, sharing your network, and engaging in microsponsorship. Each of us has the ability to make an impact through our own sphere of influence. Therefore, it's crucial to recognize the power we have and use it to advocate for and sponsor others.

An Invitation to Review This Book

In the spirit of paying it forward, please stop and review this book if you're enjoying it and finding value in the material. Simply go to the platform where you purchased it to leave a review. There is no better way to support an author than to leave a positive review, as these reviews help books rank better on the platforms that sell them and give potential readers more insight on what they can expect to learn—otherwise the book can disappear into oblivion. Thanks for paying it forward for me and other readers who will benefit from its insights. My hope is that our grassroots efforts will bring this message to millions of women, who will benefit from stepping into their authentic power.

Unleashing the Next Chapter

If you have ever received feedback or simply feel the need to enhance your communication skills in order to reach new heights of professional success, the next chapter is tailor-made for you. Get ready for a transformative journey where you will discover why owning your voice has been a struggle since childhood and learn how to break through these barriers to express your ideas with clarity, confidence, and conviction, so that you can persuade, negotiate, and influence. It's time to eradicate diminishing language that undermines your credibility and instead harness the force of your voice to captivate attention and attain buy-in from key decision-makers. Unleashing the power of your voice is the pathway to realizing your wildest professional aspirations and will help you secure your seat at the table.

BOLD Actions to Evoke Your Transformation

1. Based on your results from The DIVA Method® Get Promoted Savvy quiz, what's one area from The DIVA Method® that you most need to focus on to advance in your career? If you're not delivering results, start there. Otherwise, choose the area (image, visibility, or advisory board) where you see the biggest gap.

2. What could potentially stop you from taking action in this Get Promoted Strategy (GPS) for your career? Do you have any limiting beliefs that can get in your way?

3. What will you commit to doing to move forward?

4. ***Intersectional reflection questions:*** *Is there an aspect of your identity or a personality trait, such as introversion, that you believe will impact how you are viewed or your ability to build a strong advisory board? What proactive steps can you take to address it?*

5. What support do you need to follow through?

6. Who will you ask for help from, and who will hold you accountable for your actions?

CHAPTER SEVEN

DIVAS COMMUNICATE POWERFULLY

It took me quite a long time to develop a voice, and now that I have it, I'm not going to be silent.

—*Madeleine Albright, former US Secretary of State*

"Kisha, I'm so annoyed that I didn't share this idea first," Meghan said during our coaching session. Her frustration was so palpable that I could feel it through the Zoom screen. Meghan was one of the most thoughtful and insightful people I knew and had a similar reputation in her organization.

She explained how she'd had a great idea to share in her extended team meeting at work, one that could potentially revolutionize how they were approaching a specific marketing segment. As she'd thought about sharing her fantastic idea, anticipation had bubbled within her but doubt had begun to creep in.

"I was so excited about the possible impact of this new approach, but as the meeting progressed, I thought that maybe this idea was too far-fetched. What if my manager thinks it's impractical? Maybe I would just wait to gauge my other teammates' recommendations first, and then I would share at just the right moment. I didn't want to interrupt the flow of the discussion, anyway. While I was debating how and if to share my thoughts,

Luke started to share his perspective. And the more he spoke, the more I realized he was sharing the same concept I wanted to share."

As soon as the words had come out of Luke's mouth, Max, their manager, had begun to rave about what an innovative idea Luke had, and the entire discussion for the rest of the meeting was to unpack Luke's breakthrough idea.

"I was annoyed with myself for missing this opportunity. I could've been the one to be recognized for the value I brought, but due to my hesitation in speaking up, I missed my moment."

Have you ever missed an opportunity due to hesitating to communicate or not communicating effectively? I can relate to this experience myself, and it's something I've observed as a recurring challenge among the brilliant women I've had the pleasure of coaching throughout the years. There's often a tendency to hesitate when it comes to speaking up, sharing our thoughts, and expressing our unique perspectives, especially ones that are disruptive. Unfortunately this hesitation leads to our contributions being overlooked or undervalued, limiting our potential for growth and advancement. This leaves us feeling frustrated because we're perceived as not being leadership material, and this perception traps us in a perpetual cycle of operating significantly below our capabilities.

In this section, I will explore some of the reasons that contribute to women not owning their voices and provide practical steps to help you overcome this obstacle.

The Reasons We Don't Own Our Voice

How We Were Raised

The messages we received from our parents, family members, and society gave us an internal blueprint of how we were supposed to behave in the world. In my own Jamaican culture as a child, I frequently heard from the adults in my life that "children are to be seen and not heard." My Latina friends have shared with me that they were told, "Calladita te ves más bonita," which means, "you look prettier when you're quiet." The effect of these types of harmful narratives reverberate well beyond childhood and persist into adulthood, acting as invisible obstacles that hinder us from owning our voices.

Imagine spending the first eighteen years of your life practicing being invisible and self-silencing because of cultural conditioning. Then, suddenly, you enter the workforce in your early twenties and are expected to express yourself confidently and assertively. My colleague Elaine Lin Hering wrote the book *Unlearning Silence: How to Speak Your Mind, Unleash Talent, and Live More Fully*, unpacking this learned silence masterfully—add it to your must-read list. If speaking up confidently has been challenging for you, be gracious with yourself as you work on reprogramming your mind and developing this new habit of owning your voice.

Initially it might be hard to discard a deeply ingrained habit of being the "nice girl" who doesn't ruffle feathers. But I promise you that, with consistent practice, it will get easier and become more natural. As you cultivate the practice of unleashing your voice, allow the power of impactful communication to be your vehicle of liberation from a system that seeks to stifle your self-expression. Refuse to conform to this system; instead, use your voice as an instrument to reclaim your inner strength and fearlessly express your authentic self.

Cultural and Religious Norms

The culture in which we're raised gives us subtle and not-so-subtle messages about who we should be and how we should act. We're given messages to be nice, cooperative girls rather than intelligent, vocal, grown adult women with a perspective. Unfortunately, this cultural conditioning continues to influence how we interact with others and whether we choose to truly own our voice. To do so, we must first give ourselves permission to have a perspective.

The cultural norms regarding women's roles vary based on the region you come from. These expectations heavily influence how women show up in that region. Additionally, religion plays a significant role in determining whether women feel empowered to express their opinions and assert themselves.

American actress and broadcaster Sherri Shepherd, a former host of the talk show *The View*, expressed how painful her early years of being on the show were because she was not used to sharing her perspective. Despite being part of a TV show that expected her to speak up, she struggled with it significantly. Shepherd revealed that she was raised as a Jehovah's Witness, taught not to question the religious leaders, and accept their words as absolute truth. As a result, she did not allow herself to think critically and have different perspectives from the various messages she heard around her, both inside and outside of her religious context.[1] This made it incredibly challenging to share her opinions on *The View* because she wasn't used to independent thinking and didn't have well-formed perspectives. During those early years, she had to invest time in learning about the US political system and then forming an opinion about current events before she could use her voice to share it.

Her story is another example of how aspects of culture—specifically religion—can impact how we show up in the world around us. I encourage you not to blindly accept any norms that dictate how you should act but to reflect upon them and their impact on who you are today, then make a conscious choice on what you decide to believe and how you will behave in light of these new beliefs. Perhaps nothing will change, but at a minimum, ensure that you're intentionally choosing what to think and developing perspective by engaging critically versus just accepting a narrative as gospel truth—no pun intended.

Fear of Rejection

Fear is a topic we have explored multiple times throughout this book. I bring it up once more to underscore the significant influence it can wield over us, affecting our actions in multiple areas of our lives if left unchecked. The fear of rejection is a reason we're hesitant to share our voices. Many of us think that to be loved and accepted, we need to conform. We think that we need to adopt the same opinions as those around us and avoid being different. Consequently many of us would rather conform than risk being rejected.

Not Wanting to Be the Center of Attention

Our reluctance to speak up often stems from a fear of being the center of attention. We prefer to stay hidden in the background and not be seen because we're afraid of the responsibility that comes with visibility or the criticism that may stem from it. The weight of being in the limelight can be overwhelming, as it exposes not only our strengths but also our flaws. We fear falling short of the expectations of others and not wanting to disappoint them, especially when we're in the spotlight.

On the other hand, if we exceeded expectations by doing something amazing that gave us massive visibility, we fear not being able to replicate that result. Being in the spotlight invites criticism, as others may disagree with our perspective and proceed to criticize, judge, mock, or ridicule us. A quick glance at social media provides ample evidence of this phenomenon.

All of these risks may tempt us to remain in the shadows. However, the truth is that we have no control over what people will say when we capture their attention. There are no guarantees. Nevertheless, I firmly believe that the potential impact of using our voice for good in the world outweighs the risks associated with it.

Wanting to Avoid Backlash from Speaking Up

When we dare to step outside the box and play bigger than we have ever before, not everyone will like it; there may be a backlash that comes from presenting a different perspective. The faster we accept this, the quicker we will be able to focus on developing the resilience and determination needed to keep going despite challenges. Imagine the liberation of reaching a level where you can use the opposition that you were once afraid of as a force to fuel your tenacity. How empowering would that be? Yes, you will have opposition; this is the reality of anyone who is doing anything noteworthy in the world, especially a woman.

However, in the words of Lisa Nichols, "Don't dim your light to make other people feel comfortable. If they cannot handle your light, give them some shades." Better yet, let them go and buy their own shades! Let other people's opinions of you and their reactions to you be their business, not yours.

Mindsets to Find and Own Your Authentic Voice

Now that we've examined the cultural conditioning that has gotten in the way of owning our voices, let's shift our focus to the mindset needed to break free.

You've Earned the Right to Be in the Room, So Speak Up

You're here in the room, so exhale and release any doubt that you don't belong. Own the fact that you've been invited to the table for a reason, so pull up a seat. Don't wait for anyone else to validate you; validate yourself. Adopt TV producer Shonda Rhimes's belief that "I belong in any room I enter," and make it a personal affirmation. Allow your inner DIVA to take center stage because she has undoubtedly earned the right to be here. People need to hear your voice and unique perspective.

Your full authentic self may be the catalyst needed to challenge the status quo, push for change, and inspire innovation. Don't allow fear to hold you back and cause you to squander this opportunity. Recognize that you deserve your seat at the table just as everyone else in the room does, and seize this moment of opportunity that's right in front of you.

Understand the Value You Bring

Now that you recognize that you've earned your seat at the table and understand the importance of stepping up and using your voice to share your perspective, it's vital to understand the value you bring. Take a few minutes right now to ground yourself in the feedback regarding your strengths that you completed in the image exercise from the previous chapter. Reflect on the feedback, internalize it, and fully recognize and appreciate your strengths by regularly reminding yourself of them. It's important to not only embrace these strengths but to take steps to nurture and develop them further.

Be Authentic

In chapter 2, we extensively explored values as the foundation of our authenticity. When it comes to having an authentic voice in communication, it's important that we consistently align and ground ourselves in our values. This ensures that we stay true to our authentic selves instead of yielding to the external pressures of societal expectations. Communication is an external manifestation of who we're being on the inside. Therefore, it's important that we turn inward to remind ourselves that our authentic value lies in our qualities that differentiate us, not conforming to something we're not. By recognizing and honoring our uniqueness, we can communicate with authenticity and integrity.

Engage in Critical Thinking

I shared about Sherri Shepherd in this chapter—that is, her discomfort with expressing herself that stemmed from two root causes: the need to build expertise in US politics and permitting herself to have a viewpoint beyond her religious context. Shepherd's problem of not even allowing herself to have a perspective came from the belief that a person in authority should tell her how to think.

To overcome a challenge similar to what she was experiencing, it's crucial to cultivate an inquisitive mind that questions everything, including unchecked assumptions and messages imposed by others. This allows you to develop the ability to think independently and form your own perspectives. Rather than passively absorbing information and conforming to prescribed ways of thinking, as sophisticated women, we have the power to actively filter the information we accept by using our critical thinking skills so that we can develop our own unique understanding of the world.

Speak Up Early—It Sets the Tone

A powerful hack to push yourself to be more vocal in meetings is to be one of the first to speak up, as it establishes the tone for your participation throughout. If you wait until the very end to speak, as many who are nervous do, you may end up stressing out about it for the entire meeting and likely never say anything. I've found that if you take the leap earlier on, you're less apprehensive because you've eliminated the waiting period. To further prepare, engage in some pre-meeting work. Think about two to three points that you want to make, and rehearse them by talking out loud.

Read, Listen, and Then Reflect

Developing our own perspective can only happen if we dedicate time to reading and listening in order to expand our knowledge base. However, the process shouldn't end there. It's equally important to process and reflect on the information we've absorbed. This balance between consuming information and reflecting upon it is fundamental to the process of finding our own voice. It's at this intersection that we're able to shape our unique perspective, which fuels the expression of our thoughts and opinions.

Invite Silence and Solitude to Access Your Internal Wisdom

To effectively process and reflect on what we've consumed, we require space in the form of silence. This involves pausing our constant consumption and busyness and allowing ourselves to think and process. In a hyperconnected world where we're bombarded with data, disconnecting, befriending silence, and embracing solitude are keys to accessing our own internal wisdom, which will be the basis for forming our own perspectives.

Sometimes we spend so much energy trying to get perfect answers by gathering input from everywhere, but when we sit still and look within, we realize that the answer has been inside us all along. Dan Millman, in his book *The Way of the Peaceful Warrior*,[2] says brilliantly that we should stop gathering information from outside ourselves and start gathering it from the inside. When we take the time to look on the inside, we may discover that we already have all that we have been looking for right here within us.

Change Your Definition of Success

When we're building a new skill, such as learning how to effectively use our voice, it's important to consider how we measure success. For instance, the first time I ran a half-marathon, my objective was simply to finish. It didn't matter how much time it took—the goal was just to get across the finish line. However, once I completed my fifth marathon, my goal shifted because I'd already become pretty good at running. Therefore, I set a new target: finishing a half-marathon in under two hours. The same principle applies to improving our speaking skills.

We should not expect perfection right from the start. We need to give ourselves permission to be imperfect and take small steps toward mastery. When I coach women on speaking up and finding their voice, success at first isn't about winning over an entire room in a heated debate. It's simply about mustering the courage to speak up. If you struggle to participate in meetings but manage to share your perspective once or twice, that's a big accomplishment worth celebrating. It represents a significant milestone for you. Once you've mastered these initial small steps, you can then aim for more advanced measures of success.

Have a Perspective

One mistake that people make is merely transmitting the information or data they've gathered for a meeting. However, most of the time, the value you add comes from sharing your own interpretation of what that data means. Often, people hide behind data without sharing their opinions on what is going on because they don't want to be wrong or ruffle feathers. It does take a level of confidence, as there is a risk that the audience you're speaking to may disagree with your conclusions, but if you don't share your perspective, you're definitely not adding any value and might as well have just emailed the information to the attendees rather than show up and mechanically repeat what they can read independently. Nobody wants to be part of that meeting—it's boring and a waste of time. Don't be boring.

Stop Seeking Permission

One of the main obstacles to building our self-trust and self-confidence is our excessive concern about other people's opinions and waiting for their agreement. If you're going to be a trailblazer and launch into uncharted territory, you cannot wait for people's approval. They may not resonate with your vision, but the vision is yours, not theirs, so own it! Connect with your own desires, and move forward without waiting for others to cheer you on. The truth is that the right people will eventually follow if you're consistent and confident in what you're talking about. You don't need everyone's buy-in—just buy-in from the right people. And the first person's buy-in that you need is your own!

As you embark on the journey of discovering and embracing your unique, authentic voice, a world of endless opportunities awaits you. This development process can be an exciting adventure as you enhance both your mindset and skill set. While it may require you to occasionally step outside of your comfort zone, the reward will ultimately outweigh any temporary discomfort.

I can say with certainty that you value personal growth and development since you've made it this far in the book. Whenever you feel the discomfort of stretching yourself, remember to anchor yourself in your higher value of growth, and you will find fulfillment in this transformative journey.

Business Case Unleashed

Effective communication is critical to an organization's success (improved collaboration and more revenue).

Effective communication improves internal collaboration and facilitates better problem-solving and decision-making. This leads to improved operational efficiency, cost savings, and ultimately increased profitability for the company. By prioritizing the development of strong communication skills across the company, leaders can create a more cohesive, agile, and high-performing workforce, contributing to a positive company culture that top talent is attracted to. Furthermore, the ability to convey a company's value proposition, negotiate effectively, and handle customer interactions with clarity and diplomacy will directly impact an organization's revenue streams and overall business success.

Top Communication Traits

There are many different components that determine whether someone has outstanding speaking skills. Here are some top communication traits that you can incorporate into your communication style in order to increase effectiveness over time.

Conciseness: Speak in Headlines, Not Paragraphs

I'll never forget this statement that a member of the board of directors for a corporation made to me about a C-suite female leader whom I was coaching. "Kisha," he said, "this woman is brilliant at what she does, but her board updates overwhelm us. She spews out so much information at such a rapid pace that it's not clear what the main message or the ask is. My advice to her would be to speak in headlines, not paragraphs."

I thought that this was the perfect example of the importance of clear and concise communication. In today's digital age, where we're bombarded with information and our brains need to process vast amounts of data, you only have a few seconds to pique the curiosity of your audience before you lose them. When we speak in headlines, as we would see on a billboard or the front page of a newspaper, this compelling language grabs the attention of your audience, making both you and your message stand out.

Confidence: Know Your Stuff

The fastest way to detract from your credibility in your communication is to be perceived as not knowing your topic well or not having taken the time to do your homework. However, when you can demonstrate a deep understanding of your subject matter through effective communication, you will be able to engage your audience and build trust because you've established yourself as knowledgeable, competent, and someone worth listening to.

Customization: Tailor Your Message to the Audience

One of the marks of a highly effective communicator is their ability to tailor their message to the audience they're addressing. This demonstrates mastery of the subject matter and social awareness that will help you gain respect, foster engagement, and build rapport with the audience. This is an example of a great synergy between EQ and IQ because you strike the right balance between knowing your stuff and connecting with your audience. The more senior your audience is, the more you will need to speak in headlines; a junior audience will care more about the details.

Consciousness: Read the Room

Having social awareness is a critical aspect of being an effective presenter because you cannot establish a connection with an audience that you cannot read. It's essential to pay attention to the energy in the room, as it allows you to detect when interest is waning, a concept is unclear, or your message isn't resonating. This awareness enables you to pivot your approach, ensuring that you're staying relevant and connected with the people in the room. I've witnessed presenters stumble, not because they lacked preparation but because they couldn't adapt their strategy based on real-time cues from the audience. The ability to read a room helps you stay present and aware while remaining flexible throughout your presentation.

Confidence: Own the Room

Owning the room signals that you have full command of a space—you project embodied confidence, hold the attention of the audience, and convey authority in a natural and authentic way. As a result, you're perceived as having control over a particular situation or environment. The way each person owns the room will vary, as it depends on their ability to captivate and fascinate others by leveraging their distinct combination of strengths.

Canniness: Intentionally Utilize Nonverbal Communication and Body Language

Effective communication extends far beyond mere words. Although spoken content is important, nonverbal cues such as body language and the tone of your voice can make a bigger impact on how your message is received, how you resonate with your audience, and the level of credibility that you convey. It's crucial to ensure that your body language, facial expressions, and vocal tone are all aligned with the message that you're delivering in order to be persuasive and impactful.

Conversational: Be Easy to Engage

One of the best ways to connect with an audience, particularly at the executive level, is to be conversational and natural in your approach. I routinely remind my clients, when speaking to senior executives, to simply be themselves since they're communicating with normal human beings. When we're nervous, we can become stiff and lose our personality, but if we can remain relaxed and composed when presenting, our personality will shine through. This allows us to establish a powerful connection with the people in the room. It's important to note that being conversational and natural doesn't mean being nonchalant or unprofessional. It's about striking the right balance between being authentic and maintaining a high level of professionalism.

Catalytic: Be Inspiring

In the corporate space, many people focus on sharing information efficiently. However, incorporating inspiration into your communication can greatly enhance your impact and help you stand out. You can infuse inspiration into your communication by carefully choosing your words and employing an engaging delivery style, such as storytelling, that emotionally connects with your audience and motivates them to take action.

Even those with a more introverted style can find ways to inspire without being overly animated. If you struggle to access inspiration in your communication, it may indicate a lack of passion for your work. When you genuinely care about a topic, it becomes easier to convey conviction and inspire others. That's why passion is a powerful tool for enhancing your speaking ability. If you want specific strategies to stop getting overlooked and succeed as an introvert at work, download the guide with the same name on my website: https://www.yourpowerunleashed.org/bookresources.

Composed: Harness the Power of the Pause

Using strategic pauses in your presentations is a fantastic technique that can make a significant impact. It demonstrates confidence and control because you're not rushing through your speech. When you're nervous, you may tend to speak quickly, but incorporating well-timed pauses shows that you're at ease. This also allows the audience to digest and absorb your words. Surprisingly, pausing can enhance the power of your message by showcasing your expertise and willingness to take the time to make an impact. To truly captivate others, don't be afraid to embrace pauses. It gives your message the opportunity to resonate deeply in the audience's minds.

Clever Reasons Women Use Low-Power Language

In the final section of this chapter, we will look at communication detractors, specifically focusing on what we frequently refer to as *low-power language*. However, before we dive into the specifics of rectifying these communication mistakes, there is something that we need to address.

Women are regularly criticized for not using assertive language at work, which is seen as a sign of a lack of confidence. Over the years, there has been extensive discourse regarding the impact on women's careers of using this less powerful language. It's widely believed that these speech patterns can hinder their ability to influence others and demonstrate executive presence. However, we rarely discuss why these language habits develop in the first place and why they're so difficult to change.

Women use soft language, at times unconsciously, because we have to be savvy in our ability to navigate a complex corporate workplace system that was neither created nor designed for us to win in. Whether we realize it or not, as women in the corporate work setting, we frequently use low-power language, not because we lack confidence but because we've strategically figured out how to be heard in an environment that penalizes women for communicating with power.

According to research[3] done by Robin Lakoff, a professor of linguistics at the University of California, Berkeley, women are more likely than men to use tentative, indirect, and hedging language. This style of communication is called low power because it doesn't assert dominance or authority in the same way that more direct and forceful language might. While this information holds some truth, the bigger question is: Why does this communication style persist?

Many senior and C-suite leaders make the mistake of assuming that these language patterns indicate a lack of confidence in women without looking at the complex social and cultural norms that women need to navigate that penalize them for being assertive. Interestingly these same women exhibit different communication styles in other contexts, including outside of work or in discussions where they feel psychologically safe. It's crucial for us to explore the underlying reasons behind these linguistic tendencies. I suspect that they intuitively recognize, based on their own past experience or how they have observed other women treated in the workplace, that they must adjust their communication style in order to be heard. Additionally, we must acknowledge the intersectionality of race and gender and the specific challenges women of color experience when trying to balance assertive communication as leaders with ensuring that they are perceived as friendly and approachable.

A Black woman, for example, knows that she is often entering into a context where people may have the preconceived notion that she is angry or overly aggressive. She, therefore, strategically makes an intentional effort to smile and use nonthreatening language in order to subtly assure everyone that she is not confrontational but, in fact, cooperative. The objective in these situations is to put the other parties at ease, build rapport, and establish trust, as she is proactively trying to overcome conscious and unconscious biases in her interactions.

These women may have had well-meaning, nonminoritized male mentors who have coached them to walk in the room with swagger like they own the place, as one leader told me with conviction and enthusiasm. While they are advised to speak with power and authority, they are keenly aware that adopting the same approach as their white male mentors will not be received in the same way. This is why in chapter 9, I delve into the reasons why male leaders need to employ gender-aware coaching strategies if they truly want to support women's advancement in the workplace. Women understand that they are likely to face negative consequences and be unfairly labeled as angry, difficult, or uncooperative. In other words, they know that their peers and leaders are not ready for *their* type of swag!

If you're a woman of any background in the corporate space, you already know that it's really exhausting to have to navigate conflicting advice and expectations in order to be successful in the workplace. This, coupled with the compounded impact of bias, is a significant factor contributing to the increasing number of women in general, and Black women in particular, leaving the corporate world to start their own businesses. Despite their best efforts, it feels insurmountable to overcome these biases in order to advance professionally. Women of different racial backgrounds, including women of color and white women, face penalties for being too assertive in their communication, as it goes against cultural gender expectations.

Asian women face their own challenges, as they are commonly seen as good workers, quiet, nice, and passive, but not viewed as having great leadership potential. Author Jane Hyun coined the view of being a worker bee rather than a leader through the term *bamboo ceiling* in her 2005 book, *Breaking the Bamboo Ceiling: Career Strategies for Asians.*[4] When Asian women step up to use more assertive language, they frequently experience a bias backlash. They are suddenly viewed as hard to get along with, bossy, too task focused, and difficult.

At one financial services organization where I was employed, I had a meeting with a Korean American female leader. Prior to the meeting, I was warned that she was really "witchy," so I needed to make sure that I had all the supporting evidence for any claims that I was making. When I finally met with her, I admit that she was no-nonsense, direct, and challenged every assertion I made, but after a while, the pushback stopped, and I assume this was after she felt comfortable that I'd done my homework.

I left that meeting thinking that I didn't observe any difference between the discussion I had with her and any of the white male leaders in that organization. I expected to have all my supporting material ready for any discussion I was leading and ready to back up all my claims. I couldn't help but wonder if her race and gender played a factor in how she was viewed. At this early stage in my career, I didn't have the level of insight or vocabulary to give words to the bias I witnessed, but it was another example of how difficult it is for a woman of color to walk this tightrope and get executive-level communication just right as we manage cultural and gender biases.

Have you ever been told that you need to be more assertive in your communication style in order to have a greater impact? If so, congratulations! You're being encouraged to use a preferred influencing style that's likely not authentic to you. Here's the thing—there are many ways to influence a desired outcome. However, in the corporate world, especially here in the US, we overindex on one style, which is the extroverted, dominant norm commonly associated with many nonminoritized male leaders. Depending on the audience and the context, however, other styles may be more effective.

The most successful influencers understand how to adapt their styles to resonate with their audience and strategically choose their communication approaches accordingly. If you've ever witnessed a leader relying solely on their authority to push for something without involving others and observed that it didn't yield the desired results, you're already aware that this approach doesn't always succeed. The truth is, walking in and wielding your authority through very direct language may not be the best way to achieve your desired outcome. If you consistently use this style without considering the specific situation, you may find yourself falling short in terms of your ability to influence others at work. To assist you in becoming more strategic in your communication and avoiding the pitfalls of a rigid influencing style, here are some instances where using less forceful language can be advantageous.

Strategic Motives for Not Using Power Language

You may decide not to use powerful or assertive language when the following occurs:

- You're building trust and rapport as someone new in your role or the organization.

- You have a more senior title than the person you're interacting with and want to provide psychological safety for them.

- You strategically decide to remain quiet to assess the other parties before you show your hand.

- You're intentionally utilizing other influencing styles[5] beyond power, such as being inspirational, that you know will be more effective in helping you drive an outcome.

On the other hand, there are legitimate times when you, as a woman in leadership, should be communicating with power—but due to fear or social conditioning, you play small in your communication style because of a lack of confidence or internalized oppression. Here are some common signs showing that you're shrinking back rather than stepping up to the opportunity of utilizing powerful communication.

Signs You're Shrinking from Using Power Language

- False humility: shrinking or hiding your brilliance so that you don't intimidate or offend others.

- Wanting to be liked: you resort to people-pleasing rather than owning your voice.

- Perfectionism: fear of saying the wrong thing, so you say nothing.

Whether it's socialization, working in a hostile environment, a lack of communication skills, or internalized oppression that has gotten in the way of your ability to use your communication skills to influence effectively in a professional environment, I encourage you to utilize this chapter to help you identify the root cause so that you can take your professional effectiveness to the next level. You don't have to wait for someone to give you permission to step up and use your voice. You can take the first step today to discover your authentic voice and then own it.

Now that we've addressed the context in which women may use low-power language and when it can be strategically used to their advantage, let's turn our attention to the common communication detractors.

Communication Detractors

Detractor 1: Apologizing Excessively

I went to a very prestigious hospital when I lived in Boston a few years ago and was taken aback by the number of times the female physician apologized to me. She apologized for having to send me to get weighed, for taking my blood pressure, for asking me questions so that she could come up with a proper diagnosis, and so on. This excessive apologizing confused me and made me think she was a very new doctor. I certainly didn't want to be her guinea pig. I eventually asked her if these weren't standard procedures for all patients. When she confirmed that they were, I shared with her that there was no reason to apologize. Saying "I'm sorry" too much can create the impression that you did something wrong or are unsure of yourself. This language can raise doubts regarding your competence.

Detractor 2: Being Overly Grateful for Everything

In the same way that saying sorry and apologizing display insecurity, so does being overly grateful for everything that someone in your organization does for you. It's important to remember that you're working for a business, and the actions someone takes to help are not solely out of the goodness of their heart (although this may indeed be part of their motive). Colleagues are just doing their job for the betterment of the company, as you are doing yours.

Accordingly, be professional and be a decent human being by saying thanks for the help, but don't go overboard. Taking it to extremes can create a power imbalance or imply that you feel subordinate to others. As my proudly Jamaican aunt Becky would say, "Girl, stop it! Yuh a gwaan like yuh nuh used to nuttin' good." (Translation: Girl, stop it! You're acting like you're not accustomed to receiving good treatment.)

Detractor 3: Expressing Doubt and Hesitation

Using language such as *I think, maybe, sort of,* or *perhaps* introduces uncertainty in your language and undermines the credibility of your message. This language can unintentionally diminish your authority and give the false impression that you have not spent time doing your homework, despite your extraordinary diligence and work ethic. When you employ this form of low-power language, you run the risk of being dismissed or having attention diverted from you to someone less deserving and knowledgeable.

Resist the urge to preface statements with this language, no matter how uncomfortable it may feel. Additionally, using phrases like "I'm not sure if this is the right answer but . . ." will weaken the impact of your words. Eliminate this pattern and ask yourself why you're saying them in the first place. If you're using this language because you're trying to protect yourself from the consequences of providing misinformation, you can address this concern by stating it as an option to explore. For example, you can say, "I suggest we consider the following option."

Detractor 4: Asking a Question versus Making a Statement

In her book *Playing Big*,[6] Tara Mohr talks about how women use questions instead of statements when they are afraid of coming on too strong. Many women fear appearing aggressive, which leads them to disguise statements as questions or end sentences in a high, questioning tone of voice. These communication habits convey uncertainty or a need for validation. As mentioned earlier, social norms discourage women from expressing their strength and confidently standing by their beliefs. Release the concern that you will be perceived as a jerk, and start speaking with assurance. After all you have the expertise and experience to back it up!

Keep in mind that there are tactful ways to assert yourself without being annoying, some of which are highlighted in the upcoming table. Initially, we may encounter undesirable reactions when we confidently express our power through bold communication, but as we consistently use our newfound voice, it becomes the norm over time, and those around us will adjust to our new standard. Don't back down as you build this habit.

And while you're at it, I will tell you what I used to say to a teenager I used to mentor: "Take that high pitch out of your voice, and put some bass in it, sweetie."

Detractor 5: Using Question Marks

Adding an interrogative phrase to the end of a statement, such as saying, "I did a good job on that presentation, don't you think?" is a way of seeking validation or approval from others. However, instead of relying on external validation, it's empowering to validate yourself. Build the habit of celebrating your efforts and achievements more frequently, as illustrated by step 6 (applause) in the 6A Spiritual Practice for Courageous Women discussed in chapter 5. By recognizing and appreciating your own accomplishments, you won't feel the need to seek validation from others because you're already abundantly giving it to yourself.

Detractor 6: Avoiding Eye Contact and Weak Body Language

Have you ever been in the presence of someone with weak body language patterns, such as slouching or avoiding eye contact? If so, what was your impression of them? Without exception, when I see this, it gives off an unprofessional and even incompetent vibe. Furthermore, when anyone purposefully avoids making eye contact, it creates the perception that they're hiding something or lacking in confidence. Consequently, people who consistently avoid eye contact may be viewed as untrustworthy by others.

Detractor 7: Inserting Filler Words

Vocal fillers such as "um," "like," and even "and," when used too frequently, can indicate a lack of confidence and unprofessionalism. These are also known as *muletillas* in Spanish—for some reason, I really love this word, and I wanted to include it here if for no other reason than to show that I know some advanced Spanish words! It's important to be comfortable with pausing and utilizing silence, as it conveys a sense of calm, confidence, and control over the conversation.

Detractor 8: Minimizing Achievements

Downplaying accomplishments by using minimizing language—like "It was nothing!"—or attributing success to luck or external factors rather than acknowledging the impact of your skills and abilities is linked to one of the twelve habits that get in the way of women advancing at work—specifically the reluctance to claim your achievements, according to women's leadership expert Sally Helgesen.[7] This could be false humility at play, and it would be helpful to ask yourself why you have trouble bringing attention to your success. It may be tied to one of the reasons why we don't own our voices as women, as explored earlier in this chapter. Whatever the reason, lean into courage, step outside of your comfort zone, and begin to own, acknowledge, and celebrate your achievements. If we want others to recognize our accomplishments, we must first recognize and value them ourselves.

See the table below for examples of low-power language (or inhibited language) and how to unleash it.

Power-Inhibited Language	Power-Unleashed Language
I'm sorry, I totally missed that.	*Thanks for highlighting.*
I think . . . *I believe . . .*	*My recommendation is this . . .*
If you don't mind, I wanted to share.	*Here's the most recent information I have.*
If it's not too much to ask . . .	*I would prefer . . .*
Does that make sense?	*Let me know if you need clarification.*
I'm sorry—it's my fault/mistake.	*Great catch! I will make the changes.*
I'll try to.	*I will.*
Maybe?	*Here's another option . . .*
Just wanted to follow up.	*When can I expect an update? What's the ETA?*
Do you agree?	*Here's my recommendation.*
In my opinion . . .	Eliminate the words and make the statement.
This is the best option, right?	Eliminate the question. *This is the best option.*
We will regroup on this in the conference room, okay?	Eliminate the question. Let's regroup on this.

Final Thoughts on Communication

Executive or leadership presence and a free bonus chapter download!

Throughout this book, I have frequently mentioned executive presence because it is crucial for those aiming to climb the ladder to senior leadership positions in their careers. This intangible skill significantly influences your professional trajectory. Although the criteria many organizations use to gauge who has executive presence is laced with unconscious bias, certain things remain true. Your communication style shapes how others perceive you—whether as credible, compelling, influential, or persuasive. Effective communication is key in demonstrating your leadership capabilities and in inspiring others to rally behind your vision. It is also how you build or break connections with others that will determine whether they feel they can trust you.

Bottom line, communication is the distance between you and everything you have ever wanted, both in business and in life. If you've reached a point in your career where you know that you need to elevate your leadership presence, I've dedicated an entire bonus chapter to this topic, offering you practical steps to cultivating this seemingly elusive quality. This chapter will guide you in honing your executive presence to command respect, radiate confidence, and exercise influence, all while being your authentic self and leveraging your difference as your differentiator rather than something you have to cover or hide. For information on how to access this chapter, please refer to the resources section of this book or visit https://www.yourpowerunleashed.org/bookresources.

Making Communication Changes Stick

As you work on unleashing your power in your communication, you may feel some apprehension regarding how others will receive you. Remember you have a resource, the inner coach, to help give you the wisdom and the fortitude to stay the course. If you need to go back to the inner DIVA visualization in chapter 2 to be reminded of that power and to access your inner coach, do it as many times as necessary.

Finally, changes take time so be gentle with yourself. Try to make one small improvement daily by focusing on one habit that you want to change at a time. It probably took twenty or more years to learn to communicate the way you do today; you will not change overnight, so be graceful and patient with yourself. As author James Clear says, small, consistent changes over time can lead to remarkable results.

Tara Mohr, in her book *Playing Big*,[8] offers three additional steps that I think are key to implementing these changes:

1. Get a buddy: In chapter 4, I talk about accountability as a strategy to break through self-sabotage. Team up with someone to hold you accountable to improve in this area.

2. Record yourself: As someone who has dozens of videos of myself for the world to see on YouTube, I know this one can feel cringey, but there is no better way to catch your undermining communication patterns, including nonverbal ones.

3. Keep being yourself: You have a secret sauce that makes you captivating and fascinating, which I dive deeper into with the bonus chapter on executive presence. In your attempt to improve, don't lose that, because YOU are the secret sauce to your success!

BOLD Actions to Evoke Your Transformation

1. What is a message you received during your childhood—whether from your parents, culture, or religion—that has negatively impacted your ability to confidently own your voice?

2. Are there any other fears or belief systems that have limited your ability to speak up? If so, list them.

3. Which of the Mindsets to Find and Own Your Authentic Voice will you choose as your source of inspiration to encourage you to speak up? Which will you use as a practical strategy to aid you in speaking up more this week?

4. *__Intersectional reflection questions:__ As a woman navigating diverse intersections of identity, how do you think you have had to modify your communication style in the past to be more palatable to others in the workplace? What have been the upsides and downsides of making such adjustments? Has personality trait, such as introversion, affected your ability to be impactful in the workplace? If so, how? Based on the insights you have gained from this chapter, what changes will you make moving forward?*

5. Which one of the top communication traits does your favorite speaker utilize? What makes this trait effective for them?

6. You can go to my website to download a cheat sheet on diminishing language and refer to it daily to assist you in eliminating these common blunders from your verbal and written communication. Focus on removing one communication detractor at a time. Remember, you've spent a lifetime building these various habits, so you will not change them all at once or overnight.

7. Join an organization like Toastmasters International to help you improve your communication skills.

Unleashing the Next Chapter

The next chapter will help you develop the mindset, confidence, and master-level strategies needed to negotiate your salary and be paid your worth. Get ready to learn to navigate the art of negotiation with finesse and authority. You will be equipped to authentically advocate for yourself and receive the appropriate recognition and rewards for the value you bring. So come with me, and let's get that money, honey!

CHAPTER EIGHT

DIVAS GET PAID MORE VIA SALARY NEGOTIATION

If I had to define the gender wage gap, I would define it as the financial manifestation of sexism in our country.
—*Mandi Woodruff-Santos*

In 2022, a freelance recruiter caused a stir on social media when she revealed that she had offered a candidate a salary that was $45,000 below what the company was actually willing to pay for the role. Her explanation for this decision was that she had simply given the candidate the salary they had initially asked for, and the recruiter didn't have the time or resources to coach the candidate on salary negotiation. This post quickly went viral across various social media platforms, intensifying the ongoing discussion surrounding pay transparency and equity.[1]

When I saw this viral post, it solidified my firm belief that companies with integrity should not rely on their employees to negotiate their own salaries. Instead, they should take proactive measures to offer equitable compensation to both new hires and existing employees. The practice of shifting the burden of salary negotiation onto employees only perpetuates pay inequities, manifesting in what is commonly referred to as the *ask gap*.

Backlash for Negotiating Salary Results in the Ask Gap

The ask gap contributes to a systemic issue where women and marginalized individuals tend to ask for lower salaries, resulting in offers that are significantly lower than those extended to their white male counterparts.[2] This disparity in salary expectations and outcomes is influenced by societal norms that punish groups viewed as having a lower status for asking for too much. As a result, these groups react by lowering their compensation expectations, which leads to the unjust payment of lower salaries to women, even when their qualifications are comparable to those of men.

Research shows that women are penalized for making the case for being paid a higher salary.[3] This problem is exacerbated for women of color. On one end of this spectrum are Black women, who are stereotyped as being too aggressive and penalized as a result. On the other end of the spectrum are Asian women, expected to be meek but receiving backlash[4] when they dare to advocate for themselves.

For example, I had a Chinese American client with whom I worked to negotiate a salary increase, and the initial response from the manager was that of utter shock. He was taken aback by her request, became defensive, and shut down the discussion with her. She told me that as an Asian American woman, she was expected to be passive and agreeable—and he didn't expect her to have the audacity to advocate for herself. She believed this was the reason for his reaction.

I coached her to continue the conversation in a calm yet firm way, and after a few discussions where she presented a compelling business case on why she deserved the salary increase, she successfully obtained it. As a top performer, her expectation to be compensated in alignment with her significant contributions should not have been met with such resistance. According to Negin Toosi, a psychology professor at California State University, East Bay, and a diversity expert, these kinds of experiences revolve around status. The issue lies not in the capabilities of women or people of color themselves but rather in how they are treated when they advocate for a higher salary. Their work is often undervalued, leading to an unfair disparity in compensation.[5]

As a DIVA, you have likely begun building your advisory board, a valuable resource to leverage as you embark on the salary negotiation process. Speak with your mentors, sponsors, and coaches who comprehend the challenges and nuances of negotiating with intersecting identities. Their advice, support, and advocacy will prove invaluable in helping you navigate the negotiation process effectively and confidently, tailored to your specific needs and circumstances. By tapping into their expertise, you can craft a compelling strategy that showcases your value and strengths, thereby bolstering your position at the negotiation table. With their advocacy behind you, you can present a persuasive case with authority and clarity, maximizing your potential for a positive outcome.

Companies should actively engage in pay equity audits to address wage disparities. Undertaking such audits not only demonstrates their ethical commitment to doing the right thing but also brings mutual benefits to both the organization and its employees. The burden of earning a fair wage commensurate with role, level, and performance, regardless of gender or other demographic markers, should not be placed on the employee but is the organization's responsibility. Leaders should not shy away from salary discussions with their employees, especially strong performers that they want to retain.

Instead employers should be prepared for a robust discussion where both parties decide on a course of action that's well supported by a solid business case. When approached in the right manner, salary discussions can serve as valuable developmental opportunities for both managers and women negotiating their salaries. These conversations provide leaders with a chance to enhance their conversational intelligence by engaging in difficult discussions, offering direct feedback, setting clear expectations, and coaching employees to present strategic business justifications instead of dismissing the conversation altogether.

Simultaneously employees are challenged to participate in the discussion with a focus on the strategic value they bring to the organization rather than purely personal gain. My hope is that both leaders and employees will feel empowered to be transparent during these discussions rather than avoid them. Salary negotiation is a dignified discussion and should be treated as such, allowing for open and respectful communication.

Now that I have emphasized the importance of recognizing that salary negotiation should not rest on the shoulders of employees and is indicative of a larger organizational culture issue, I maintain my empowered stance of not waiting for the system to self-correct. Unfortunately many organizations (I hope not yours) will not proactively do so. While we're not in control of the initiative that a company decides to take, we do have our own ability to negotiate for ourselves. Unlike the viral freelance recruiter mentioned earlier, I do have the bandwidth to teach you how to negotiate your pay! So let's get into it.

As per our usual practice, we prioritize addressing mindset before delving into the tactics of any strategy. This is particularly vital in a society that undervalues the contributions of women. Unfortunately not only do you have to work through your own internal challenges with money, but the problem is compounded by having to power through external obstacles designed to keep you in your place. Considering these challenges, it's crucial for you, as a highly compensated professional, to cultivate a mindset of abundance rather than scarcity.

The Mindset of a Highly Compensated Professional

Everyone at all levels of an organization should be fairly, equitably, and generously compensated for their contributions. Therefore, it's essential to internalize the understanding that you're truly deserving of substantial reward for the value you bring to your company. Your work has a significant impact, which directly contributes to the organization's profitability. Consequently, you rightfully deserve a share of these profits.

Many women are very uncomfortable with conversations around money, and they shy away from these discussions or avoid them altogether. The first thing I want to tackle is shifting your thoughts and energy around money. If you believe that having money is evil, then you will consistently sabotage yourself into being underpaid or will squander whatever pay you do get above what you think you deserve. This is an energetic thing, so we need to work on increasing our vibrational financial frequency.

In order to have positive energy around money, I recommend four things.

1. Be grateful for the money that has flowed into your life so far and how it has supported you, your family, and your experiences with loved ones—for example, taking a vacation and being able to contribute to causes you care about.

2. Ensure that your money does good. Instead of buying into the narrative that money is evil, which sabotages your financial health, just make sure your money does something positive. When good people are financially

prosperous, they can use that money to bring "more good" into the world. Align your financial decisions and investments with your values to decide what causes you want to support. This could be social justice, environmental sustainability, tithing in ministries, or supporting disadvantaged communities through educational programs. Whatever the cause, it should be an area where you want to make a positive impact.

3. If you're like many women who feel more comfortable advocating for others than you will for yourself, then use purpose-driven motivation as your guiding principle. Reframe your negotiation conversations as doing it for the greater good of women, including your daughters, nieces, or mentees. Eliminating the gender pay gap starts with you.

4. Use money mantras to reprogram your thinking. By repeating these money affirmations or creating your own, you will replace negative or limiting beliefs with positive ones and reprogram your subconscious mind by creating new neural pathways that program positive change.

Here are some affirmations that I love:

1. I am a good person, and good people should have a lot of money because when good people have abundance, we can do "more good" in the world.

2. I am richly compensated for the value I bring.

3. I effortlessly attract money, which multiplies and grows.

4. I am grateful for the abundance that is already present in my life.

5. I am excited to receive more abundance in all its forms, including a higher salary.

Vision Board

A bonus tip is to visualize yourself as financially prosperous; because if your mind cannot see it, you will never achieve it. Gather pictures of what being financially prosperous will provide for you, the experiences it will give you, and the contributions you will be able to make, and put that on a vision board to look at daily. This will reprogram your subconscious mind to receive instead of resist financial wealth. You can use either an online vision board or a manual one. Check out the resources section to see some recommendations.

Salary Negotiation Skills: Get That Money, Honey

The only way to receive higher compensation is to practice the negotiation golden rule: always, always ask. The good news is that after decades of being told that we don't negotiate enough, the tide is finally turning. New research[6] shows that women are beginning to ask for more compensation, and after reading this chapter, I hope many more of us will join this trend.

Prerequisites for Negotiation

Here are a few things to keep in mind before you start the salary negotiation process:

Listen and Understand

When it comes to negotiating, we think about how effective we need to be in speaking, but listening is an overlooked secret weapon. Listening well allows us to gather information, build rapport, display empathy, and discover hidden interests. Sometimes just by listening well, we will be able to win in a negotiation because most people are not heard at a deep level. Listening may earn you the favor of others wanting to work with you to fulfill your requests.

Focus on Value

Salary negotiation is a dignified business discussion, not a charity. Therefore, it must always be tied back to how it will benefit the company. If you're not adding value based on your strong performance in this role, there is no business case for a salary increase.

Let Go of Fear—Especially of Not Being Liked

In chapter 4, we talked about fear being a reason we shrink from stepping up and going after what we want. Review this chapter to practice ways to deal with these fears. The fear of rejection and criticism, which is connected to wanting to be liked, are all fears that can block us from engaging in salary negotiation. Remember, you have friends and family who like you already. What you're going after right now is equity and respect. This is also another opportunity to access the power from your inner coach through doing the inner DIVA visualization again.

Mind the Relationship

Women are inherently relational. We strive to be collaborative and build rapport with others. Use your listening skills, body language, and tone to preserve the relationship and inform the way in which you negotiate. Maintaining relationships isn't about not asking for what you want—it's how you go about it that matters.

Feminine Energy: Negotiate Like a Woman

As we delve into the tactical steps of salary negotiation, let's address an important misconception: the notion that successful negotiation requires adopting a stereotypically masculine approach. This belief suggests that traits such as competitiveness, a win-lose mentality, and aggression are better suited for negotiations, while feminine energy and traits are undervalued. However, Cindy Watson challenges this notion in her book *The*

Art of Feminine Negotiation and encourages women to intentionally bring their overlooked "feminine" traits to the negotiation table. By embracing these qualities, women can enhance their negotiation skills and increase their chances of success.[7]

I agree with Watson's assertion. If your authentic style aligns more with what would be considered more typically feminine traits like collaboration, empathetic listening, intuition, relationship building, or open and transparent communication, leverage these natural skills to your advantage during negotiations. Embracing these qualities will set you apart and challenge conventional patterns. There are many ways to win—not only one—so use your unique feminine advantages in the way you negotiate.[8] Your femininity is not a liability but an asset. So unleash your power to negotiate like a woman!

Here are the critical steps that we need to take as we embark upon the salary negotiation journey.

Salary Negotiation Steps

Step 1: Do Your Homework First

It's important to do your research on the pay range for the type of role you're seeking and aim for the top end of that range during negotiations. This is because negotiations often result in a downward adjustment. However, it's equally important to determine your walk-away number, which is the bare minimum you're willing to accept for the role. To gain a better understanding of the market range for the job, consider reaching out to recruiters from other organizations and conducting additional research.

I've noticed that many women, including myself and those I coach, feel more confident to negotiate more effectively when armed with data about what their peers are earning. In one job, for example, I found out that my white male counterpart with less experience was making $10,000 more than I was. This gave me the confidence I needed to advocate for myself. As they say, knowledge is power, and this knowledge reassures you that you're taking the right steps.

Here are some resources that you can use in your pay research:

- **Online Salary Databases:** Various websites such as Glassdoor, Salary, and Payscale offer free access to salary information for a wide range of professions, industries, and geographic regions. You can use this information to benchmark your desired or current salary against industry averages to determine whether you're being paid fairly.

- **Job Postings:** Job postings for similar positions in your industry can offer insights into the salary range for that role. You can also use this information to gauge the level of demand for your skills and experience.

- **Professional Associations:** Many professional associations conduct salary surveys or offer salary information for their members. This can be a valuable source of information for negotiating a pay increase. If you're in the US, some examples of associations that conduct surveys are the Society for Human Resources Management, the American Institute of Certified Public Accountants, and the National Society of Professional Engineers.

- **Your Network, Friends, and Family:** You can also ask colleagues you trust, mentors, or other professionals in your network about their salary ranges or salary ranges for roles they manage if they are leaders. This can give you a sense of how much others in your field are earning and help you negotiate a fair salary.

- **Company HR Department:** You can also speak with your company's HR department (some HR professionals will share, some won't—but you won't find out unless you ask) or your manager to get information on the salary range for your position within the company. This can provide you with a baseline for negotiating a pay increase.

- **Public Sector:** Some government entities post their salary information online. Visit the official website of the municipality or state government you're interested in.

You can use the information from these sources to make a compelling case for a salary increase when you combine it with emphasizing your contributions to the organization, your skills, training, and experience. However, be realistic and self-aware about your level of performance. If you know that your performance is subpar, this is not the time to negotiate. Instead get your performance up so that your employer will be incentivized to pay you more.

Business Case Unleashed

Salary negotiation benefits employers too (retention of top talent). Providing competitive compensation to employees is not just a cost but is an investment in a company's success. When employees are fairly rewarded for their hard work, they feel valued and motivated to stay with the company, which directly impacts retention rates, reduces turnover costs, and strengthens the employer's brand. However, embracing and encouraging a culture of value-driven compensation negotiation takes it a step further. It demonstrates that the company recognizes its employees' contributions to the business' success and is committed to rewarding them for it in an equitable way. This not only fosters a culture of trust and respect, but also enhances the employees' sense of ownership and accountability for their role in driving the business forward.

Step 2: Prepare a Brag Bank

Before initiating a salary negotiation conversation, it's essential to prepare a comprehensive list of your accomplishments. This document will serve as evidence of the value you bring to the table when discussing salary with your boss or hiring manager. Highlight instances where you've outperformed the average, such as showcasing cost savings, process improvements, increased efficiencies, enhanced team engagement, or any other relevant data that supports your exceptional contributions. Providing concrete evidence of your outstanding performance will strengthen your case during the negotiation process.

As part of your evidence, you will want to create a brag bank, which is a folder with emails, notes, or documents from clients, coworkers, or leaders that corroborate your claims. Ensure that you provide as much quantifiable data as possible, such as numbers and facts. The special notes from the leaders will typically be more qualitative in nature and are good material to show the impact of activities that cannot be easily quantified. In today's work environment, where improved employee morale, engagement, and emotional intelligence are essential to thriving organizations, having evidence of the qualitative nature of your accomplishments in addition to the quantitative ones can set you apart.

Step 3: Adopt a Business-Oriented Approach

I once worked with a client who was generating substantial revenue for her company but wasn't receiving due recognition. We discussed various strategies for her to effectively communicate the positive impact she had on the business and the value she brought. It's important to remember that when advocating for fair compensation, this isn't a favor that others are doing for you. It's ultimately a business decision, and you should approach it as such by highlighting the tangible benefits and value you bring to the organization.

Step 4: Plan the Right Timing

Use timing to your advantage. You'll want to start planting seeds of your expectation of a salary adjustment three to four months before your annual salary review. If you wait until the performance season has started, it will be much harder to get an increase, because by then your boss may already have an idea of what they want to pay you, and the budget for the team may already be locked in. If you start the conversation early, your salary expectation will be the anchor, not what they think you deserve. And your boss will be able to advocate to HR or finance as to why they need a larger budget during salary planning season. In salary negotiations, the party who states their salary expectation first sets the anchor point for all future discussions and, therefore, wins.

Step 5: Always Start on a Positive Note and Maintain Positivity Throughout the Process

When initiating a salary conversation, it's important to approach it with a positive and constructive mindset. Starting the discussion with positive energy helps to create a collaborative atmosphere and sets the stage for a successful negotiation. This approach not only helps alleviate any apprehension you may have about the conversation but also makes the experience more positive for the person you're speaking with.

It's worth noting that, as a woman, you may encounter a certain level of discomfort with the idea of women negotiating their salaries, even when trying to negotiate with other women who are leaders. However, don't let this discourage you from having the conversation. Rather it highlights the importance of being intentional about the tone you set for the discussion. By approaching it with a positive and collaborative attitude, you can help overcome potential biases and ensure a more productive and fair negotiation process.

Start the conversation with something like "I really enjoy the work I'm doing here (or I'm really excited to start this role) and find my scope very challenging, which pushes me to learn and grow. I've been noticing that the breadth of my contributions has expanded quite a bit and I have gotten good feedback on the impact of my work. I'd like to discuss with you the possibilities of reviewing my compensation."

Use positive statements to keep the tone constructive. For example, instead of saying "I'm not being paid enough," say "I believe my skills and contributions warrant a higher salary."

Avoid complaining, discussing other people's salaries, highlighting your workload, or mentioning financial difficulties. Instead maintain a positive demeanor and bring positive energy to the conversation. None of these other points are relevant to your boss's motives for increasing your pay. Their primary concern is the impact of your contributions on the company's bottom line. This is not charity; it's a business discussion, so treat it as such.

Step 6: Set Up a Formal Meeting and Be Professional

A salary conversation is important and should not be handled nonchalantly in the hallway or by dropping by your boss's office. Instead schedule a time to have a formal discussion and have all your accomplishments neatly typed up in the event that your boss needs to reference them. Keep those talking points conversational, but be prepared to have something formal to hand over if they ask or if the conversation goes that way.

Step 7: Know the Exact Number

According to researchers[9] at Columbia Business School, you must ask for a very specific number—for example, $94,750 rather than $95,000. When you use specific numbers in your initial discussion, it gives the impression that you've done extensive research on your market value to arrive at that number, which increases the likelihood that you will receive something closer to what you asked for.

Step 8: No Is Never Final

If you're afraid of hearing a no, recognize that a no is never final. It's just the beginning of the negotiation process. Expert negotiators say you've not started negotiating until you hear a no. Look at the no as the stepping stone to your yes. That yes can be with your current employer or with another one.

If the manager says no, instead of getting angry or disappointed, get curious and ask questions. This will keep the conversation productive. If they have not provided an explanation for their decision, ask them for one. You can say something like "Help me understand the reason for your decision," and then determine with them if there is anything you can do to influence a change of heart. For example, if there is a performance gap, get a clear explanation of what improvements need to be made to turn things around. Find out what they need to see in order to bridge any potential gaps.

If the reason is that there's no money available, suggest an upgrade in your position, like a promotion. It's easier to rationalize a salary increase when it's linked to an upgrade in job responsibilities.

Note: Never give an ultimatum. It's a small business world, so don't tarnish your brand or burn bridges.

Step 9: Be Willing to Go Where Your Talent Is Adequately Valued and Compensated

Moving to a new team or company is always an option. Many people will stay in a corporation that undervalues them and take the hard road of constantly fighting for their worth. It's much more energizing to be in a place that appreciates you and is ready to invest in you than in a place where you have to constantly prove why you deserve equal treatment. There are many organizations out there that will be excited to compensate you fairly for your performance, so be willing to move on from anyone and any company that does not value your contribution enough to pay you fairly for it.

Note: When negotiating a salary before going into an organization, pay attention to how the process is handled. It's a very good indication of how willing they will be to pay you what you're worth. If the salary negotiation process is arduous, beware. You're going to be fighting for every penny once you're hired! Decide what your walk-away point will be. Even though walking away is not easy, it's a lot less painful than working for an organization where you don't feel valued from day one.

You want to avoid putting yourself in a position where you will feel bitter. Be bold enough to say no when it doesn't feel right, knowing that you always have options at your disposal. There are literally millions of companies out there, and this role is certainly not the only one you will qualify for.

Step 10: Think Beyond Salary, Especially When You're Just Joining a New Company or Taking a Promotion

Don't ignore the value of added benefits in compensation packages. You can negotiate components such as job title, additional vacation days, relocation expenses, tuition reimbursement, training and development, professional association membership, new equipment, office space, leaves of absence, childcare assistance, participation in mentoring programs with senior leaders, travel expenses, cost-of-living adjustments, meal allowances for working late in the office, 401(k) matches, and so on.

I conclude this chapter with a story to give you hope. I had a client who desired a higher salary but was afraid to ask for it. I challenged her to do both the mindset work and take the tactical steps mentioned above in order to have a successful negotiation. Furthermore, I encouraged her to state the exact amount of money she wanted. Surprisingly, the figure she shared with me was double what I would have recommended. However, through our coaching sessions, she developed a deep understanding of the value she brought to the table, which empowered her to be audacious enough to ask for what she truly deserved. She used the salary negotiation process as an opportunity to embody her Bold, Audacious, Courageous self, which we discussed in chapter 5. Even as her coach, I must admit that the sum she mentioned stretched my own belief of what I thought was possible. But her business case was so compelling that I could not refute it.

She had a discussion with her boss—the chief financial officer (CFO), no less—who was highly impressed by her negotiation strategy and the courage she displayed. As a result, not only did her boss grant the salary increase, but she also inquired about how she had acquired such a skill. Upon learning about her experience with me, this CFO invited me to the organization to conduct a workshop for all the women in her department. The workshop aimed to teach them the principles of Your Power Unleashed.

Let this example be a lesson for you to not be scared to negotiate for what you want. A supportive leader and company will respect and reward you if you approach it in a constructive manner. The way in which you're treated throughout this process will reveal how much the organization truly values your contributions. If you're in a place that's willing to invest in you because your contributions are making a difference, you know you're in the right garden where you will bloom and enjoy a fulfilling career. If not, this is also valuable information that you can use to decide on your next best step. You're now armed with the skills and mindset of a highly compensated professional. It's time to go out there and get that money, honey!

BOLD Actions to Evoke Your Transformation

1. Which of the mindsets of a highly compensated professional (gratitude, affirmations, purpose-driven negotiation, or money doing good) will help you raise your vibrational financial frequency?

2. What is one affirmation from the list that resonates with you that you will begin to repeat daily?

3. Have you ever missed an opportunity to negotiate a salary increase? If so, which one of the salary negotiation steps would have most helped you negotiate?

4. ***Intersectional reflection questions:*** *What specific concerns do you have about how your intersecting identities could impact your ability to negotiate your salary effectively (e.g., education level, age, race, immigration status, or disability)? What proactive steps can you take to address these challenges and advocate for fair compensation? As discussed in this chapter, leverage your advisory board to support you in this process.*

5. Do you have an opportunity to negotiate your salary now? Plan on how you will negotiate using all the salary negotiation steps. Grab a friend to role-play the conversation with. Get feedback and do it!

6. Write a letter championing yourself on all the traits you already possess as a woman that will help you be a strong salary negotiator (e.g., listening skills, collaboration, open and transparent communication, integrity, directness, confidence, data research, etc.).

Unleashing the Next Chapter

Share the next chapter with a male leader you respect to guide him as he explores gender-aware coaching strategies tailored for championing women in the workplace. In this chapter, he will not only discover how to become a catalyst for change and a powerful advocate for gender equality but also encounter inspiring insights and questions that ignite profound self-reflection, empowering him to become a better coach to women. He will also learn strategies for removing bias blind spots, enabling him to become a more effective and empathetic coach to women in the workplace.

CHAPTER NINE

DIVAS SUPPORT— GENDER-AWARE COACHING STRATEGIES FOR MALE SPONSORS

Coaching is a form of professional development that brings out the best in people.

—*Elena Aguilar*

"I have already heard the premise of much of these arguments, so I found myself becoming dismissive of the content initially, but Kisha, it was my second reaction that caused me to take an honest look at myself. I found myself ready to get on the defense. It took self-awareness and intentional internal dialogue for me to put myself in an open and curious mindset to learn from this work." This was the honest reaction of Dan, one of the male executives to whom I sent a draft of this chapter.

I had reached out to Dan and a few other male leaders for their thoughts, curious about the questions it might raise for them and its overall usefulness. Despite his role as a vocal supporter of women on his team and a father who desired to see his daughters have unlimited opportunities to contribute their brilliance to the world, Dan's internal reaction to reading a chapter on what he thought was highlighting gender inequities in the workplace surprised him. His candidness with me about his initial discomfort before even turning to the second page was a testament to his high level of emotional intelligence. He was self-aware enough to name what was going on inside of him and to actively manage his reactions. This allowed him to engage with the material in a way that would be helpful for his goals as a leader.

This is not easy work. It demands an awareness of our defenses and discomforts, understanding their origins—such as past unproductive conversations or media narratives—and choosing to push past them with a greater goal that compels us to act. Some male leaders admit to feeling annoyance or even fear of accusation when gender equity discussions arise. However, we all recognize that progress requires confronting this discomfort and navigating the complexities to reach our intended goals.

As Dan reflected on his reaction, he offered a perceptive observation: "In business we face hard situations every day and address them as leaders of our organization so that we can solve or overcome them to achieve our objectives, financial or otherwise." He resolved to treat this situation similarly. If it's hard, I am just going to do it hard, I do hard things every day. I am a leader; it's what I do. He said that once he put himself in the mindset to be ready to tackle and look at whatever challenge was presented, with an empathetic yet solutions-oriented approach, he was ready to go. For Dan, this challenge transcended revenue targets; it was a matter of simply doing the right thing.

So now I extend the same invitation to you. As you read this chapter, you will encounter both familiar ideas and new perspectives. You may agree with some and not with others. Some ideas will inspire you; others will stretch you. Regardless, I encourage you to approach this content with an open and curious mind, ready to engage and to become an agent of change. Together, let's explore how we can foster workplace cultures that empower women and individuals from all backgrounds to thrive.

***

Women make up only 28 percent of C-suite positions, which means that men occupy at least 72 percent[1] of the decision-making power, authority, and influence in corporations. Despite these numbers, when experts discuss ways to shatter the glass ceiling, men are mostly left out of the equation. This makes it appear as if gender equality is only a women's issue. It's not. The truth is, if we're going to make substantial progress in achieving gender equality, it will need to include a partnership with men, who are the most underutilized resource in this endeavor.

I've spent eight chapters coaching and equipping women to own their power, but it would be irresponsible to ignite their inner fire to shatter their internal glass ceiling while ignoring the external challenges women face. Unfortunately this is where many women's leadership programs in corporations fail. These programs encourage women to "lean in" but fail to prepare the organization to fully embrace and support the newfound empowered mindset of these women. Women then face backlash, which leads to feelings of disillusionment, frustration, and in some cases, even attrition.

Dismantling an oppressive system is both an internal mindset endeavor as well as an external systemic and culture work. Since both men and women play a role in keeping the system alive, this book on unleashing your power would be incomplete if it didn't also call men forward, especially those in positions of power, to step up as partners in the mission. The truth is that all business leaders and executives, regardless of gender, should prioritize gender equality. This commitment is not only ethically sound but also a strategic business decision. Embracing diversity, including gender equality, as supported by various studies conducted by organizations like the consulting firm McKinsey, leads to improved financial performance, fosters a culture of innovation and creativity, and enhances employee engagement and retention. These outcomes ultimately drive increased profitability and revenue growth.

I've met male leaders at all levels of corporations who are fully invested in the development of the top talented women on their team. However, they naively try to coach women without taking into consideration the unique challenges they face when they attempt to step into their power in a corporate environment that isn't always ready to embrace strong, decisive, female leadership. They underestimate or are unaware of the repercussions women encounter when they step into their power and are uncertain about their role in the conversation about gender equality.

The purpose of this chapter is to educate and equip male leaders who want to create an environment in their organization where the best talent can flourish regardless of background. These leaders are ready to rise up to partner with the women on their teams and their female peers in leadership to drive gender equality forward, taking into consideration intersectional realities of women of diverse backgrounds.

In my corporate experience, when female leaders advocate for gender equality, they are frequently penalized more harshly than men.

Research backs up this experience by showing that men are able to avoid the ramifications women face,[2] and the higher this male leader is in the organization, the less likely he will be to encounter any backlash to his allyship. For this reason, I know that it will take all of us, especially men in the most senior leadership positions, not just half of us, to bring this system down. To this end I invite all the women who are reading this book to share this chapter with the men on your advisory board or other male managers, mentors, and executives.

In this chapter we will discuss ways you as a male leader can do the following:

1. Coach women to step into their power
2. Help remove environmental barriers at work

Solution, Part I: Coaching Women to Own Their Power

As a leader you can coach your employees to higher levels of performance by helping them break through the confidence-shattering internal barrier of self-doubt. I explore self-doubt in depth in chapters 1 and 2 of this book. You are invited to read these chapters to gain a better understanding of this phenomenon and to access the tools that will help your team navigate through it. What I will do in this chapter is help you identify signs of it at play and show what you can do about it from the position of a leader.

Here are two common scenarios that managers encounter that are opportunities to coach their employees to overcome self-doubt:

Scenario 1: You have a high-potential employee on your team, and you put her on a stretch assignment that would give her visibility to various senior leaders. But at every turn, she checks in with you to ensure that she's taking the right steps on the project. She has great instincts, but in this project she's overly dependent on you and doesn't trust herself, which is slowing down her progress. After much probing, you realize that she is dealing with self-doubt about not being as smart or experienced enough to take this work on.

Scenario 2: You have a strong performer on your team, who in one-on-one meetings clearly articulates her rationale for the work she's done. But when she goes into larger meetings, she's very quiet even though you know she has valuable insights to add. She eventually confesses to her teammate, who tells you that she feels her accent is too thick—so people won't understand her—and this self-consciousness makes her hesitate to communicate in larger settings.

These two examples are evidence of your employees dealing with symptoms of self-doubt, and as a leader, I know you've had similar experiences where you saw strong performers not fully step up into the potential that you see in them. In my own experience as a midcareer employee, I had a manager (who mistakenly interpreted my silence in meetings as a lack of confidence) tell me that I needed to walk in the room with more swagger.

"Don't wait to be invited," he said. "Insert yourself."

Essentially, he was telling me to lean in.[3]

What he didn't know was that I had a *lot* to say, and I didn't lack the confidence to say it. The issue was that I was hesitant to insert myself because based on prior experience, I was well aware of the backlash that I could receive if I pushed my perspective beyond what others were comfortable with. No matter how much I smiled in my delivery, it seemed as if my efforts would be interpreted as angry or bitchy. Most women in corporate have had at least one experience of others not being receptive to their strong perspective due to conscious or unconscious bias, so they learn to shrink. I could have told him about the time I dared to offer a differing opinion on the direction of a project and a leader used a not-so-funny euphemism about the Incredible Hulk to insinuate that I was an angry Black woman. Unfortunately Black women in particular are frequently mischaracterized as angry when simply providing feedback or expressing themselves. This stereotype is rooted in the intersection of gendered and racial biases.

Did I tell this well-meaning manager about my previous experiences? No. I was exhausted. I knew my differing perspective would bring about a better outcome, but at what personal cost? I would rather this well-meaning manager think I wasn't confident than receive the backlash of having "too much swagger." I honestly didn't feel like explaining why I held myself back and decided it wasn't worth it.

Now that I'm an executive coach, if I could do that conversation with the well-meaning manager all over again, these are the things that I would tell him to make him a better coach of women in his organization, including women of diverse backgrounds.

The first thing this manager needed to know was not to assume why his employee was quiet in meetings. He needed to get curious and engage in a coaching conversation to find out her rationale rather than diagnosing it. Coaching is one of the best tools that leaders can use to develop their team and be a multiplier[4] of talent, and curiosity is one of the most important skill sets of an effective coach. However, it's not enough for managers and leaders to develop generic coaching skills; they need to specifically develop gender-aware transformational coaching skills.

Gender-Aware Transformational Coaching Skills

Coaching, according to the International Coaching Federation, is "partnering with clients in a thought-provoking and creative process that inspires them to maximize their personal and professional potential."[5] The effect of coaching is to unlock a person's untapped abilities so that they can reach their self-defined goals. As a coach, I wholeheartedly believe in and have seen the transformational effects of coaching in helping others break through their own internal barriers to reach levels of achievement that they have always dreamed about. I also understand that there are external obstacles that women and people of diverse backgrounds have to be cognizant of when they move into action. Managers must be aware of what these challenges are to effectively coach women and proactively address them.

Something that managers need to be aware of as they're coaching women is that the same behaviors that are viewed as strong leadership qualities in men are customarily viewed negatively when displayed by women. In fact, when women, and especially diverse women, display these qualities, they are repeatedly penalized.

One very clear example that's common is the misinterpretation of assertiveness. Assertiveness in a woman is often interpreted as aggressiveness or bitchiness, and she is penalized if she doesn't manage not being seen as a wallflower versus being seen as difficult, or angry if she is Black.

As a manager, when you're not aware of these nuances, you may interpret your employee's reluctance to implement the strategies you've given her in mentoring sessions as a lack of confidence or even think that she's swung the pendulum too far when you get feedback from others on "how she behaved." This awareness will allow you to give nuanced coaching to your employees and challenge the system (other decision-makers) when you hear feedback that alerts you to underlying biases.

Eleven Leader Blind Spots That Limit Their Ability to Effectively Coach Women

The following are common misconceptions that your female team member may encounter, ones you should be aware of as her leader coach:

1. Assertiveness: When coaching women on your team to be more assertive, it's crucial to be mindful of the potential negative reactions they may face.[6] Assertiveness in women is regularly misinterpreted as aggression or bitchiness, while the same behavior in men is seen as strong leadership. As a leader, you should actively challenge and address the inconsistent standards and biased assessments that occur when women exhibit assertiveness as compared to men.

2. The Likability Penalty: As you coach her to be more direct, be aware that directness in women can trigger an assessment penalty because she isn't viewed as likable. This is a blind spot for male leaders since likability isn't typically a factor when discussing male performance. Successful women need to employ various ways to overcome this form of gender bias.[7] The way to deal with this as a leader is to challenge this idea of whether it's important for her to be likable versus effective, and if this is also an expectation for men.

3. Too Emotional: When women display strong emotions such as frustration or anger, they are labeled as overly emotional or sensitive while men are considered passionate or assertive. When women are labeled as emotional, it diminishes how legitimate people perceive their arguments[8] to be, and it undermines their credibility.[9] Again, actively challenging inconsistent standards among the genders is key.

Additionally, if there is truly a development opportunity here, use your leadership coaching skills to support your employee to improve her self-regulation, which is an important aspect of emotional intelligence. This will help her manage her hot buttons (which many men struggle with as well).[10]

4. Negotiation: When a woman negotiates, especially for her own benefit, as in the case of her compensation, she's frequently viewed as too demanding and less competent than her male counterparts.[11] Men, on the other hand, are viewed as confident and competent when they negotiate. As a result, women are often punished, and even though new research shows that women are more likely to ask for more pay, they still earn less than men.[12]

Make sure women in your organization are encouraged and affirmed when they negotiate instead of penalized.[13]

5. The Motherhood Penalty: Being a mother has a negative impact on a woman's career because leaders assume that mothers are not as driven or ambitious to climb the corporate ladder. As a result, she may be offered fewer opportunities or promotions, and she will earn a lower salary than fathers and nonmothers.[14.] Research has in fact shown[15] that American workers experience mothers as having stronger leadership skills than working fathers or employees without children—in being calmer in crisis, more diplomatic, and better team players. As a leader, don't make assumptions about a mother's career aspirations or willingness to take on projects and roles, but do create an open-door policy where she will feel safe expressing her desires and needs.

6. Her Physical Appearance: Physical appearance, including clothing, makeup, weight, and hair, is often disproportionately scrutinized for women. Hair is particularly an issue for Black women, who experience hair discrimination at work,[16] illustrating the intersectionality of race and gender challenges for women of color. To address this, ensure that performance conversations with all employees, including women, are focused on skill sets and abilities rather than physical appearance. Leveraging competency models that focus on objective, observable, and measurable skill sets, behaviors, and attributes that are critical for success in their roles can help minimize any tendency to overemphasize physical appearance.

7. Overlooking Intracultural Biases: Even when men are of the same culture, race, or ethnicity of the women they mentor and have shared experiences based on that commonality, it's crucial to consider the intersectionality of gender and be aware of the potential for discrimination against women within their own demographic. In the Black and Brown communities, issues such as colorism (preferring lighter skin tones over darker ones) and biases related to hair texture (preferring straighter and smoother hair over curlier or kinkier ones) can contribute to disparities in professional opportunities for impacted women.

Machismo, an exaggerated form of masculinity, is one that my Latina sisters often describe as affecting the way men of their culture interact with them and perpetuate discriminatory behavior, even within professional settings. Men who come from similar backgrounds as the women they interact with, particularly from marginalized communities, must engage in more deliberate self-reflection to understand how their cultural perspectives shape their interactions with women. This is the first step in a man's journey to be an ally who will actively work to dismantle ingrained prejudices and discriminatory behavior, while advocating for gender equality within their cultural context.

8. Age Discrimination: This type of discrimination affects women in distinct ways, subjecting them to harsher judgment as they grow older, when it is assumed they'll be retiring soon, which limits their access to various opportunities. Conversely, when women are perceived as too youthful, their knowledge and credibility may be questioned. These contrasting views create challenges for women at different stages of their careers.[17] As a leader, ensure you're making employment decisions such as hiring, promotion, or placing people on important projects based on their skills, not age, and being an advocate when you see these issues at play.

9. Not Technical: Women in technical fields such as engineering, information technology, and so on are often viewed as not technical enough just because they are women. I heard this frequently when I was a HR leader from managers, but when I probed for evidence for this assertion, especially compared with their male counterparts, there was usually nothing substantive. When you hear these statements as a leader, probe for data to substantiate these claims.

10. Office Housework: Women—and in particular, women of color—are regularly asked to do office housework,[18] be the clean-up crew, plan events, run errands for meal takeout, take meeting notes, and so on. And if they refuse, they're viewed as not being team players. These activities don't lead to career advancement; however, glamour work leads to visibility and promotion. As a leader, you can ensure that office housework isn't forced on women by having a rotating schedule where everyone takes their turn doing this type of work[19] rather than allowing it to default to the women on your team.

11. Buying into the Meritocracy Myth:[20] Although coming from a good place, meritocracy is counterproductive to eliminating bias. As I explain in detail below, if you want to build an environment where all can succeed, leaders must challenge themselves to examine all decisions with a critical eye rather than assuming they are merit based so that they don't miss blind spots that exacerbate bias.

As you initiate coaching, mentoring, or sponsoring relationships with the women you lead, being aware of these blind spots can help you coach them in a nuanced way and work with them to develop savvy strategies to be successful at work despite the blind spots. Whether or not you name these specific blind spots, the women on your team are likely already thinking about them, so it's best to address the elephant in the room.

Realize that, as a leader, change should start with you. So, as you read through the blind spots, identify the ones you've been holding—even if subconsciously. Challenge your own perceptions by thinking critically about these areas and engaging in constructive conversations with those who think differently than you because they have had other life experiences. These actions will allow you to broaden your perspective and expand your frame of reference. Realize that the strategies that worked for you might not work for women because they can receive backlash that you would not as a man, even if you came up in the same company.

Meritocracy: A Damaging Myth and a Blind Spot

"Kisha, I don't care about gender, race, or any other identifier. My focus is who the best performers on my team are and are they getting the support they need to excel? I'm going to hire the best. I'm a big advocate of diversity, and I believe in meritocracy."

These were the words of a very self-assured senior leader who worked in an organization I was consulting for. As a former employee of General Electric in the Jack Welch and Jeff Immelt eras, I was very well versed in the mindset of the meritocracy manager.[21] Unfortunately this well-intentioned sentiment is completely counterproductive to building the best teams, and it breeds more bias than if the leader or organization did not pride themselves on valuing a merit-based culture.

Research[22] shows that those who think they're the most objective often exhibit the most bias because they don't monitor their own behavior for biases. Biases proliferate in these situations because individuals are not actively taking steps to manage their blind spots, and as a result of this lack of diligence in auditing their decision-making processes, more opportunities for unintentional partiality are created. When organizations emphasize meritocracy, it reinforces a belief of impartiality, which creates the prime scenario for both implicit and explicit biases to be present.[23]

The bottom line is if you want to reduce the risk of bias, approach all employment decisions with a critical eye, scrutinize the situation, and ask others to help assess for bias.

To create equal conditions for all employees to excel, we must be diligent to insert counter perspectives so that we can expose blind spots that feed biased behaviors and decisions. Operating under the assumption of pure merit leads to complacency in efforts to identify and eliminate bias, so we must remain persistent in our commitment to uncover and eradicate bias from our processes and practices.

Now that we have identified significant blind spots that may hinder your effectiveness as a coach for the women on your team, let's explore the powerful role of coaching in the context of gender-aware leadership development. Women bring diverse perspectives, experiences, and skills to an organization, and when these attributes are harnessed effectively, they can drive innovation, enhance decision-making, and improve overall team performance. Women inherently contribute to the improvement of businesses, so let's examine how coaching can be utilized as a tool to unleash the boundless potential of women within your organization.

Coaching: Unleashing Transformation and Empowering Women

Coaching is a development tool that managers can use to accelerate transformation in their employees and enhance their own leadership skills. It does so because it puts the leader's ego at bay and promotes agency in women. When the leader takes on the role of a coach, their responsibility isn't to be the knight in shining armor who sweeps in to rescue their employee with their knowledge and expertise. Instead the aim is to build capacity in the employee themselves. To facilitate this process, the leader needs to be curious about what challenge the employee is experiencing and hold them as capable of solving their own problems with appropriate support.

This kind of curiosity involves active listening and resisting the urge to fix or solve on behalf of the employee. It involves embracing intellectual humility, acknowledging that this person is the one best equipped to generate solutions for challenges they encounter—with you, the leader, acting as coach. The leader learns alongside the employee as they partner to co-create a way forward. This is true empowerment because they are essentially teaching this person how to fish for themselves, which requires no mansplaining, saving, or rescuing! When leaders engage in coaching, they must remember that women need to be supported, not saved.

The collaborative nature of coaching is effective because people are much more likely to engage with solutions that they come up with themselves as opposed to those told or directed at them. When they have actively contributed to the solutions and therefore feel a sense of ownership, they are motivated to prove themselves and others right. This increased buy-in and motivation leads to greater follow-through and implementation of the solutions.

Coaching with a gender-aware approach holds significant power, as it avoids placing women in subordinate positions within typically patriarchal corporate settings. Instead it establishes an egalitarian partnership that recognizes and appreciates their capabilities. It provides them with the necessary support and allyship within a system that was not originally designed to promote their success. By taking this approach, coaching empowers women to navigate and thrive within the corporate environment while maintaining their autonomy and sense of dignity.

Business Case Unleashed
The benefits of coaching and supporting women (employer brand and talent attraction).
By actively fostering a workplace culture that champions and supports women, companies attract and retain top talent from diverse backgrounds, which ignites a culture of innovation and enhances their competitive advantage. This sends a powerful signal to potential employees that the company is dedicated to cultivating an inclusive environment where every individual, regardless of their background, can thrive. This approach resonates with the values and expectations of the modern workforce, particularly among Gen Z and millennials, and establishes the company as an employer of choice for individuals from all walks of life.

Three Essential Coaching Skills of an Impactful Leader

Now that we have set the context for gender-aware coaching, let's review the three transformational coaching skills that you can use now to develop your high-performing employees. A good way to remember these skills is to know that a great coach is a PAL—which stands for powerful questions, accountability, and listening.

Powerful Questions

These are open-ended questions that spur the person being coached (referred to as the coachee) to think deeply, which creates the possibility for learning and fresh perspectives. When the coach uses a powerful question, he invites the coachee to clarity, exploration, and action. This skill allows the coachee to gain a deeper understanding of themselves and their situation at a whole new level.

As a manager, you will find the use of powerful questions helpful in a myriad of situations, including setting goals and objectives at the beginning of the year, brainstorming sessions, career development discussions, and even in execution one-on-ones. When using powerful questions, just allow genuine curiosity, openness, and intuition to guide you. A coach doesn't tell—but leads with curiosity and asks. A well-formulated question invites the coachee to think deeply and self-reflect, which can unlock innovative solutions, facilitate decision-making, and build trust and rapport.

Here are a few of my favorite powerful questions that I use in coaching conversations.

1. What is your biggest priority right now?
2. What does success look like for you at the end of this conversation?

3. What support do you need from me?
4. What are potential obstacles that you may face?
5. What part of the situation have you not yet explored?
6. Help me understand . . .?
7. What's a possibility that you've not yet contemplated?
8. What do you think is best?
9. What resonates the most with you?
10. What was the lesson learned here?

Accountability

Coaching that's transformative always ends with a commitment to take action. This action is the focus of accountability, which is holding people responsible for what they said they were going to do. This is the courageous side of coaching—you hold the person responsible for following through on their commitments so that they can stay on track with their goals. Without accountability, you're not coaching; you're just having a nice conversation. Accountability elevates the coaching conversation by providing a clear path toward goal attainment because there are consistent actions being taken toward that end.

What I love about accountability is that it increases the motivation of both the coach and the coachee. The coachee is driven to stay committed when they know they will be held accountable for their actions. Simultaneously, the coach feels inspired by witnessing tangible results from their coaching efforts. Accountability helps you balance creating a safe space (which is established through curiosity, deep listening, and rapport-building) and stretching the coachee by challenging them to grow.

I learned three accountability questions while I was in coaching training at the Co-Active Training Institute many years ago, and I still use them to this day. They are:

• What are you going to do?

- By when will you do this?
- How will I know?

Listening

One of the things that makes coaching so transformational is the opportunity for the person being coached to be deeply listened to. I don't know about you, but in so many of my daily interactions, people rarely slow down to be fully present and listen. Most people are just listening so that they can respond, impatiently waiting for you to take a breath so that they can slide in and say something. So when a person has the opportunity to be truly heard, it's indeed a rare gift. Listening at this deep level helps to create psychological safety for your employee and builds rapport with them because they feel seen, heard, and even validated.

As a manager/coach, you will observe that a lot of times, just by engaging in this level of listening with your employees, you facilitate transformation almost effortlessly. At times all that a person needs is to have a listening ear and space to process while they talk through things out loud, ultimately figuring out their own solution. The coaching conversation is great because it provides this space to process that people don't customarily get.

One rule of thumb in a coaching conversation where you're the coach is that you should be listening most of the time—at least 70 percent. The person you're coaching should be doing most of the speaking. An acronym that I teach managers to help them self-manage the amount of time they spend speaking is the WAIT—why am I talking?

The Co-Active Training Institute breaks down this skill of listening into three levels,[24] which is very helpful in guiding through the deepest levels of effective listening.

Level 1 Listening: It's All about Me

This is internal listening where you're focused on your own thoughts or perspective, what you want to say next, and your own judgment. I call it "it's all about me" listening because everything you hear is filtered through your own agenda so you're only half listening to the other person. This level is only appropriate in very few situations. The primary one is when you're being coached or mentored. In this case, you should be thinking about and prioritizing your own needs!

Level 2 Listening: Focused on the What

A deeper level of listening is focused listening, which centers on the person being coached and what they're saying. At this level, nothing distracts you; you're totally in the moment with the person speaking and even focused on information gathering. Level 2 listening is used in coaching conversations where you're working to solve a problem, brainstorm, or in execution one-on-ones.

Level 3 Listening: Beyond the Words

This is the deepest level because while your attention is still completely engaged with the person you're coaching, you're also able to perceive anything else that's going on beyond what they're saying. I refer to this level as "beyond the words" because it involves a keen observation of various cues beyond verbal communication. It includes noticing subtle changes in voice inflections, emotions that lie beneath the words, body language, and more. You pick up on the full context of the discussion and notice what is being said and what is not said. It demands the coach's full presence, requiring them to utilize their perception and intuition to pick up on subtle cues that may not be readily apparent.

Most of us do not regularly practice this level of listening in any aspect of our lives, especially in our fast-paced, distracted world, so embracing it in the workplace may feel completely foreign at first. However, once we recognize the transformative power of this type of listening in developing connections with others, we will want to develop these deeper listening habits. Level 3 listening can be applied in any situation and allows the coach to be fully committed to the agenda of their coachee. Beyond the words listening constitutes a significant portion of the listening time for highly effective coaches.

Scenario: Applying Gender-Aware, Transformational Coaching to Real Life

To illustrate an example of how these coaching skills can be used to unleash the power in women, let's revisit the advice where a leader told me that I needed to walk into the room with more swagger. Instead of assuming why I wasn't speaking up and proceeding to tell me what I needed to do, a better approach would have been for him to get curious as to why I wasn't speaking up and use powerful questions, combined with deep listening, to come up with a practical action plan to move forward. Below is a hypothetical conversation of how that leader could have been coaching me.

> Leader: Kisha, I've noticed that you've been very quiet in our broader cross-functional meetings, and I know based on our one-on-one conversations that you have a perspective on the course of action to take. Help me understand what has been contributing to your quietness.

> Me: Wow, was it that noticeable? I'm more of an introvert, and I would rather listen to everyone

else's perspective and wait until I have something valuable to say rather than just run my mouth.

Leader: That's fair, but in the last meeting when we were talking about retention, I know you had a differing perspective. And you didn't speak up until I prompted you.

Me: Well, I wasn't sure the VPs in the room were ready for what I had to say, and they were probably going to do what they wanted anyway, so I decided to choose my battle.

Leader: If I'm interpreting what you're saying correctly, you didn't speak up because you didn't think they would be open to another perspective. So this is a fight you didn't feel was worth it?

Me: Yes. I didn't think it made sense to put myself at risk for nothing.

Leader: Interesting. I notice you use the words *battle* and *risk*, which to me implies that there is a feeling of danger. Is that right?

Me: Yes. I've been in situations in the past where, when I presented a different point of view or challenged the prevailing perspective, it wasn't received well, and I received backlash and was labeled as not being a team player or being too aggressive. I don't want to place myself in that situation again.

Leader: Based on that experience, it totally makes sense that you would want to protect yourself from those repercussions. If we could figure out a way to eliminate the chances of this happening, how would you want to show up in those discussions? Meaning, what would you want ideally for yourself in these situations?

Me: Well, I would love to show up as the innovative problem solver that I am, which would require me to disrupt the current way of thinking and present alternatives that can not only help us see around corners but also create a new solution that would be best for the entire team.

Leader: I love that. I think that if you can show that you're here to disrupt ideas for a better team outcome, and that it's not personal, maybe people will be more open to listening. What do you think?

Me: That's a good point. But I've tried to do that, and it hasn't worked. The truth is that people are much more willing to engage with a guy like you challenging them than if I do it.

Leader: Okay, that's fair. If we go back to your desire to show up as the innovative problem solver, is there any support that I can provide to help you make this happen?

Me: Well, now that I think about it, I would be much more willing to disrupt if I knew I had air cover. So, if I share my perspective, and you realize a negative reaction in the room, it would help for you to display your alignment and challenge this bias behind the scenes with your peers, bringing awareness to inconsistent standards applied to men versus women and diverse people.

Leader: I commit to doing this. Are there any other action plans you've not explored? How well do you know the other VPs, for example?

Me: Well, the truth is, I don't know any of them on a personal basis. And most of my discussions with them are pretty transactional.

Leader: It seems like there's an opportunity to build relationships with them, then. And this may make them understand where you're coming from because they'll better understand your style and become open to your differing viewpoints.

Me: Good point.

Leader: I read a great opinion piece in the *New York Times* called "How Women Can Escape the Likeability Trap,"[25] and I'm going to email it to you. I think it has some great insights that other successful women in corporate have used to help them overcome this form of bias. Obviously, though, I'm also going to continue doing my part as a leader to be vigilant about addressing these biases in our organization.

Me: I would love to read that article to see if there is anything else I should be thinking about.

Leader: Also, I think Adebola Bakare would be a great mentor for you. She has been a successful SVP in our organization. We have spoken quite a bit about the challenges she has had to navigate as a Black woman and immigrant as she came up through this organization.

Me: Oh, I would love an introduction!

Leader: Okay, I will make it happen. As a result of this conversation, what action will you commit to taking?

Me: Well, first of all, I'm going to read that article that you recommended. Then I will set up time this week to have one-on-ones with at least two of the VPs and look for other ways I can build relationships with people in the room. Finally, in next week's meeting, I do have some perspective on one of the proposals Kirk has. So I will be sure to vocalize this viewpoint.

Leader: Sounds like a plan. And let's discuss your progress, learnings, and the challenges that you experience in our next one-on-one.

The above is an example of gender-aware transformational coaching. There are three things I would like you to notice as a leader from this scenario.

First, just by looking at the length of this coaching conversation, your reaction as a leader may be that this is a *lot* of hard work. Yes, it is, and can you imagine how much harder it is for a woman to have to actually walk this tightrope daily of being effective in her role while adjusting her style to deal with ridiculous biases—without undercutting her perceived competence? It's pretty exhausting all right. The outcome of this type of coaching, however, is well worth it, as it creates an environment for her to have psychological safety and build strong relationships with her stakeholders (including you) so that she can contribute to the company at the highest level of performance possible. Everybody wins.

Second, notice the use of more questioning and listening rather than telling.

Finally, there is an opportunity to share resources and some advice once you uncover the real challenge that the coachee is experiencing. Connecting her with successful female leaders, both within and outside the organization, who have navigated similar paths can provide her with an invaluable support network. The leader was also able to share an article because he invested time in educating himself to improve his awareness of challenges around diversity, equity, and inclusion. I have included quite a few references in this chapter's bibliography, especially the one on developing coaching skills as a leader,[26] which will deepen your learning.

As you proactively improve your ability to coach women on your team to own their power, it's also crucial to consider how you might challenge and improve the existing system.

Solution, Part II: Advocacy—Challenging the System

The authors of the book *Glass Half-Broken: Shattering the Barriers That Still Hold Women Back at Work* contend that "eliminating gender disparities at work is about more effective talent management"[27] and requires holistically addressing managerial practices systemically and thoroughly, not piecemeal. This is absolutely true, and since leaders are the owners and primary enforcers of these systems, it's crucial to mobilize all leaders—particularly men in this context—to proactively address bias in their organizations' people systems as a potent step to creating a glass-shattering work environment. In this final section of the chapter, I will highlight key actions that male leaders can take to support a thriving work environment for women to contribute and reach their full potential.

Challenge Bias by Bringing Awareness to Inconsistent Assessment

If you hear women being described as aggressive versus assertive, as highlighted earlier in this chapter, discuss how they are acting consistently with others in their organization but are being held to a different standard. You can start by saying something like "Are we equally applying these criteria to everyone or just to her? This person seems to be behaving consistently with how I see many male leaders behave in this company." Remember, the response from a man holding another man accountable is going to be totally different than if a woman challenges them.

Be a Sponsor

A sponsor is someone who uses their social capital to open doors for others and bring awareness of their contributions. As a leader, you can sponsor talented women in your organizations by doing the following:

1. Highlighting their work to other leaders and even higher-level decision-makers in your organization.

2. Ensuring their contribution is recognized, including restoring credit when necessary. If you notice someone else talking about the work of a woman without giving them credit, restore credit to them. You can say something as nonconfrontational but direct as "I'm glad that Maryann

shared that with you, Brad, and that you're bringing her great insights to this discussion."

3. Provide visibility to leadership opportunities. When you hear about a project or other leadership opportunities that are well within a woman's competency and expertise, insert her name. You should also nominate her for opportunities including promotions, new roles, industry events, or development programs.

4. Provide mentorship and guidance. Sometimes due to limited exposure to certain cultures, types of environments, or to certain levels of leadership, a woman—especially those of diverse backgrounds—might not understand the rules of the game (aka the unwritten rules of success in corporate spaces). If you're more skilled at this, you can be a mentor and teach them what you know so that they can set themselves up for success.

5. Introduce them to your network. Most successful leaders know that you don't just work your way to the top. Having a strong network helps you get there faster. Facilitate connections for female talent. Introduce them to influential people inside and outside the company who can help them expand their reach and open doors to new opportunities.

Ensure That Women Are Fully Integrated into the Team

When a woman is not fully included in her team, she misses out on informal conversations that help her build trust and access important information that's shared unofficially. This can make it harder for her to succeed in her role. In addition, she may not have the chance to form key relationships with influential people who could help her succeed professionally. This is why, historically, conversations on the golf course, where deals are made—and women are rarely present—are disheartening. They are emblematic of a greater problem of women's lack of access.

As a leader, you can do two things:

1. Look for organic ways for the women on your team to work toward shared outcomes with people of various demographics. Ideally, this will be happening automatically on your team.[28]

2. Ensure that women are not left out of social activities where important connections can be made.[29]

Listen to and Validate the Experiences of Women

To support women and foster a more inclusive environment for everyone, male leaders should actively seek opportunities to hear women's stories and genuinely listen to their concerns. It's essential to acknowledge that women are the experts of their own lives, so it's crucial to amplify their experiences without dismissing or diminishing their encounters with gender bias or subtle acts of exclusion

By doing so, we can cultivate psychological safety, making women feel heard and respected. Men can also create a bridge of understanding by educating other men, which can build trust within the work environment. By adhering to these principles, we can establish a workplace that values and supports women's voices.

Intersectionality: Pay Special Attention to Amplifying the Voices and Experiences of Diverse Women

As stated in the introduction of this book, intersectionality is a concept coined by scholar Kimberlé Crenshaw that recognizes that women's experiences are not only shaped by their gender but also by other factors such as their race, religion, sexuality, disability, culture, language, and so on. Gender equality and the ensuing women's leadership programs in corporations normally lump the needs of all women into one homogenous category, which fails to address the nuanced needs and experiences of diverse women. As a result, diverse women feel not only ignored and marginalized by a patriarchal society but also betrayed by feminist movements, which have historically been dominated by white, middle-class perspectives.

As you work to amplify the voices of women, be cognizant of whose specific needs are not considered, such as women of color, transgender women, older women, disabled women, those operating in a country where their native language is not spoken, and so on. Identify who is overlooked, take action to bring visibility to them, and amplify their voices.

The Invitation to Be a Change Agent and a Co-conspirator!

I end this chapter with an invitation to you as a male leader to become a change agent and co-conspirator to actively work alongside women and other gender equality advocates to challenge systems of inequality in the context of your workplace. You have the opportunity to use your power to support and give visibility to the women with whom you work.

Don't be afraid to take a stand against sexism, discrimination, and other forms of oppression, even if it makes you uncomfortable. Comfort is the enemy of progress. If you are afraid of being criticized for taking a stand, take note of something speaker and author Ben Greene once said, which is the strongest call to action I've ever heard for allies. He said that "if you are my ally and the stones being thrown at me are not hitting you, it means you're not standing close enough." This is a powerful statement from him as a transgender man. Allyship isn't easy work, but nothing worthwhile in life is. I hope you will get to the same conclusion that the leader Dan from the beginning of this chapter did. You have done hard things in many other areas of your life, so if it feels hard, good—do it hard! It's time to step up.

Conclusion

CATCHING FIRE—A MOVEMENT, NOT A MOMENT

"This movement was something so extraordinary, not only because it saved my life—... but also because it demonstrated that change was possible as a result of organized, mass pressure."

—*Angela Davis*

We've taken a courageous journey over this entire book to do the deep internal work necessary to find fulfillment both at work and in life. The truth is that when we learn to own our power in one area, it overflows into all other areas because of the metamorphosis that we go through. We've also learned savvy strategies that will help us navigate an organization with wisdom and grace so that we can make an impact that stretches far beyond ourselves, and as a result, be abundantly rewarded for the value we bring. As adults we spend the majority of our waking hours at work. Therefore, it is worth the effort to ensure we feel satisfied and accomplished in this area.

***

Congratulations for finishing this book. You are an exceptional woman. However, your journey isn't done. Unleashing our power is not a one-and-done process. It's a practice that we commit to on a daily basis so that we can strengthen our power muscles. Just as we must commit to exercising multiple times per week in order to remain fit and keep our muscles toned and strong, in the same way we need to strengthen our inner power muscles regularly and in new situations. You may have mastered your ability to tame the inner critic in your role as a financial planning and analysis (FP&A) leader, for example, but that pesky little thing shows up again when you're promoted to CFO. Remember, this isn't a reason to freak out; it just means that you're learning, growing, and being stretched outside of your comfort zone.

You're building your capacity to lead, and it will require you to embrace the lessons that you've learned in this book in a new situation and in a new way. Be encouraged, however, because you're not starting all over from scratch. You're building upon what you've already learned. If you encounter what feels like a setback, you'll bounce back faster and make a stronger comeback. Just keep coming back to the practices you've started along this journey. You will realize that you're more resilient than ever. You may encounter a hiccup, but it won't stop you from stepping up. The challenge will no longer seem like a mountain but rather a molehill.

I want you to approach this book not as a textbook but as a workbook. Now that you've read it, digest what you've learned, apply the lessons, and then come back for more. Every time you apply a lesson, especially in new situations, you're deepening that transformation at the DNA level—not because of magic but because of the scientific process of experience-dependent neuroplasticity[1]. This scientific concept is an encouragement to keep coming back to these lessons and implementing them. Over time you will do them automatically without even having to think about it.

Neuroplasticity: The Six-Syllable Word for Hope

If you think that you can never change from the woman that you are now to the one you desire to be, science disagrees with you and asserts that you can change. Neuroplasticity refers to the brain's ability to change and adapt throughout a person's life. Experience-dependent neuroplasticity takes place when we take action, such as learning a new skill or engaging in repetitive practice that causes the brain to go through structural changes via neuroplasticity. These structural changes encode transformation into our nervous system, making the brain more efficient at facilitating the execution of the skill with greater ease and proficiency over time.

A perfect illustration of this process at play is when we're driving. When we first learn to drive, it requires conscious effort and attention. However, with repeated practice and reinforcement, the neural circuits in our brain associated with this behavior become more efficient, and driving becomes automatic. This is why even after just one year of consistent driving, you no longer have to think about the mechanics of it; you just get in your car and, without even realizing it, you're at your destined location. Due to neuroplasticity, no matter what your starting point, you're capable of changing. Your brain was designed to facilitate change. Neuroplasticity, therefore, is your six-syllable word for hope.

As such, you should keep returning to this work by doing the inner DIVA visualization, maintaining a Your Power Unleashed® journal, and committing to doing BOLD Actions daily. By doing so, you're actively rewiring your entire nervous system to embrace your divine feminine power. Challenge yourself by asking, "What's the one thing I can do today that will push me outside of my comfort zone?" This is your BOLD Action. Additionally, ask yourself, "Who can I mentor in the principles of Your Power

Unleashed® to pay forward the progress I've experienced?" Every time you take action, be sure to take a moment to applaud yourself; remember, it is a key part of the 6A Spiritual Practice for Courageous Women that we discussed in chapter 5. You deserve this recognition, and equally important, whatever gets celebrated gets repeated. Celebration is an integral part of the transformation process, as it triggers the brain to release neurotransmitters like dopamine, which reinforce the behavior.

A Movement That Catches Fire

I have applied the Your Power Unleashed® principles in my own life, and it has caused me to transform in ways that I never imagined. I opened this book with the story of the performance and promotion review conversation that propelled me to bring a solution for women in an organization. I had to own the fact that there was a problem that no one seemed able to fix, and if I didn't step up to address it, no one else would. I had a vision of what could happen, but the organization didn't. It took me first recognizing my own agency and ability to bring change to that company and then owning my voice to influence others to catch the vision.

At first I spoke to my manager, but he didn't catch the vision. I had to go back to the drawing board, practice my talking points, and then go back to female leaders who I thought would get it. They caught the fire of the vision and then partnered with me to get time with the business leader to propose this Your Power Unleashed® program. I communicated my vision to the CEO, who initially seemed bored, but I was able to influence him with my talking points. I knew he'd caught the fire when he said, "This is a great idea. Forget this company. This is a big need beyond us. Go do a TED Talk."

That's when I *knew* he'd caught the fire. I still plan to do that TED Talk! A few months later, I stood on stage at a corporate event with more than 500 leaders and executives of this company and kicked off the program. People came up to me afterward, including men, asking how they could help. They, too, caught the fire. Yes, men can also be a part of supporting this movement by being advocates, co-conspirators, and sponsors.

This message has brought me to stages in places such as Brazil and here in the US, launching this program with women across the globe. They caught the fire. I finally decided that the CEO was right—this message was bigger than that firm. Women across various corporations, industries, and organizations could benefit from this message, and it was the basis of starting my leadership consulting and coaching business, which has operated for the past four years. All this transformation started with one decision to *unleash my power.*

Will you decide to unleash *your* power? If you accept the challenge to do this, your mind will be blown, just as mine was. Imagine the unbelievable possibilities that will open up to you in the process. You will also find that the impact of this mission extends far beyond yourself. What I know for certain is this: when women of purpose take leadership roles, we can drive the positive change we've been waiting for others to champion. By unleashing our power, we can dismantle biases, stereotypes, and systemic barriers, rewrite the narrative, and create a new paradigm for leadership—one that's inclusive, compassionate, collaborative, and driven by values that honor the diverse voices and talents of all.

My invitation to you is to make the decision to unleash your power daily and bring other women along with you to do the same. In doing so, you will transform your decision from a moment into a movement.

Your Power Unleashed®: The Movement

If you want to transform your decision to unleash your power from a moment into a movement like I did, here are a few things you can do so that you're not on this journey alone.

DIVA Book Club: You can buy copies of this book and share it with four of your girlfriends to form a book club and accountability group where you apply the principles of Your Power Unleashed® and commit to taking BOLD Action. You will find a DIVA book club discussion guide resource on my website: https://www.yourpowerunleashed.org/bookresources.

- **Share with Male Change Agents:** I already made the invitation in the final chapter to share that specific chapter with the men on your advisory board (the *A* in The DIVA Method®). I will repeat that invitation here and expand it to any man in leadership or peer whom you consider a change agent or co-conspirator. Men are an important part of the goal to create glass-shattering workspaces.

- **Your Power Unleashed® Program:** You can bring the Your Power Unleashed® coaching program to your company. By implementing it within your organization, you can foster an environment that creates the conditions for talented women to thrive. This program is designed not only to benefit individual women but also to impact the entire organizational system. It encompasses various components, such as providing coaching skills to managers, establishing sponsoring and mentoring programs to facilitate executive-level exposure and engagement with high-potential women, and guiding the leadership team through an organizational maturity matrix to promote women's advancement. Through our comprehensive consulting strategy, we aim to facilitate genuine systemic transformation within your organization. Contact us at yourpowerunleashed.org/contact to discuss options for your company.

- **Keynotes and Workshops:** You can bring a Your Power Unleashed® workshop (some employee resource groups for women have done so) or a keynote speech to one of your company's conferences. Keynotes and workshops can be done live or virtually. Go to yourpowerunleashed. org/corporations to learn more.

- **Teaching Future Generations:** You can mentor your daughter, niece, or other young ladies in your community, school, church, or religious youth groups on the principles of *Your Power Unleashed®*. The earlier our girls can learn these principles, the sooner they will learn to self-coach rather than self-criticize and live up to their full potential.

- **LinkedIn, Blog, and Social Media:** You can go to my blog and LinkedIn page, where you will find fresh insights and resources to equip you to unleash your power. I also post content on YouTube and Instagram, if you're active on those platforms.

- **Review This Book:** One of the best ways to make *Your Power Unleashed®* a movement is to bring more exposure to this work. Book reviews on Amazon, and so on, bring great books out of obscurity and give them visibility, which you already know is key to success. I would love to see how quickly this book can get to the target of 100 reviews, then really blow it out of the water with 1,000+ reviews, to spread its impact like wildfire. If you haven't done so yet, please help ignite this movement by reviewing this book if it has brought value to you in any way. Simply go to the platform where you purchased it to leave a review. These positive reviews help books rank better on the platforms that sell them and give potential readers more insight on what they can expect to learn. My hope is that our grassroots efforts will bring this message to millions of women, who will benefit from stepping into their authentic power.

Here is a list of the bonus resources to complement this book.

- The Inner DIVA visualization
- Rewire Your Brain for Success: How to Rewire Your Brain for Courage and Success guide
- Ten Confidence-Building Strategies That You Can Implement Now eBook
- The DIVA Method® Get Promoted Savvy quiz
- The Ultimate Promotion Checklist and Resource guide
- Managing Up: How to Get Your Boss to Support Your Career Advancement guide
- Bonus chapter on executive presence
- Stop Getting Overlooked: Succeed as an Introvert at Work
- Link to the Fascinate Test®, which is strength-based
- DIVA book club discussion guide
- Vision board recommendations

For more information on these and other programs or resources, please visit my website: www.yourpowerunleashed.org/bookresources.

Author Bio

Kisha Wynter is a distinguished leadership consultant, executive coach, speaker, author, and the innovative mind behind the DIVA Method®. Renowned for her expertise in fostering inclusive cultures within organizations, Kisha collaborates with businesses to ensure environments are created where all talent thrives, regardless of their backgrounds.

A former HR Leader for Corporate Audit Staff, Americas, General Electric's premier executive development program and expert on women in leadership, Kisha brings a wealth of knowledge to every venture she pursues. Her work spans 50+ countries and multiple industries—impacting organizations such as General Electric, Baker Hughes, Twilio, Chief, DKC, Lundbeck US, Concordia College, Nordson, and more.

Learn more about Kisha's transformative work at www.yourpowerunleashed.org and continue the conversation on LinkedIn @KishaWynter.

Kisha resides in the New York City tri-state area and enjoys the beach and learning languages.

Bibliography

Chapter One

1. Brown, Brené. *Daring Greatly: How the Courage to Be Vulnerable Transforms the Way We Live, Love, Parent, and Lead.* Penguin Publishing Group, 2012.

2. Barrett, Lisa Feldman. *Seven and a Half Lessons about the Brain.* Boston: Houghton Mifflin Harcourt, 2020.

3. Purushothaman, Deepa. *The First, the Few, the Only: How Women of Color Can Redefine Power in Corporate America.* New York: Harper Business, 2022.

4. Earley, Jay, and Bonnie Weiss. *Freedom from Your Inner Critic: A Self-Therapy Approach.* Boulder, CO: Sounds True, 2013.

5. Ibid.

6. Nichols, Lisa. *Abundance Now: Amplify Your Life & Achieve Prosperity Today.* New York: Dey Street Books, 2016.

7. Barrett, Lisa Feldman. *How Emotions Are Made: The Secret Life of the Brain.* New York: Mariner Books, 2017.

8. Clance, Pauline R., and Suzanne A. Imes. "The Imposter Phenomenon in High Achieving Women: Dynamics and Therapeutic Intervention." *Psychotherapy: Theory, Research & Practice* 15, no. 3 (1978): 241-247.

9. Leiba, Elizabeth. *I'm Not Yelling: A Black Woman's Guide to Navigating the Workplace.* Coral Gables: Mango Publishing, 2022.

10. "Gender Equality Is Stalling: 131 Years to Close the Gap." World Economic Forum. Published June 20, 2023. Accessed

November 25, 2023. https://www.weforum.org/press/2023/06/gender-equality-is-stalling-131-years-to-close-the-gap

11. Winn, Marc. "Perfectionism vs Excellence." The View Inside, February 27, 2013. Accessed November 26, 2023. https://theviewinside.me/perfectionism-vs-excellence/

Chapter Two

1. Wynter, Kisha. "Experience the Love Meditation—Love Is Greater Than Fear During Challenging Times." March 25, 2020. Video, 6:15. https://youtu.be/THiWz-c9FK4. Accessed January 22, 2024.

2. Betz, Ann. "The Power of Dreaming, the Power of Action." Your Coaching Brain, February 6, 2015. Accessed January 22, 2024. https://yourcoachingbrain.wordpress.com/2015/02/06/the-power-of-dreaming-the-power-of-action/

3. Harvard Medical School. "Relaxation Techniques: Breath Control Helps Quell Errant Stress Response." Harvard Health Publishing, July 6, 2020. Accessed January 22, 2024. https://www.health.harvard.edu/mind-and-mood/relaxation-techniques-breath-control-helps-quell-errant-stress-response

4. Elrod, Al. The Miracle Morning (Updated and Expanded Edition): The Not-So-Obvious Secret Guaranteed to Transform Your Life (Before 8AM). Dallas: BenBella Books, 2023.

5. Hanson, Dr. Rick. Hardwiring Happiness: The New Brain Science of Contentment, Calm, and Confidence. New York: Harmony Books, 2013.

Chapter Three

1. Covey, Stephen. The 7 Habits of Highly Effective People. New York: Free Press, 1989.

2. Hewlett, Sylvia Ann. Executive Presence: The Missing Link between Merit and Success. New York: Harper Business, 2014.

Chapter Four

1. Barrett, Lisa Feldman, PhD. "Try these two smart techniques to help you master your emotions." June 21, 2018. Accessed November 24, 2023. https://ideas.ted.com/try-these-two-smart-techniques-to-help-you-master-your-emotions/

2. Jiang, Jia. "What I Learned from 100 Days of Rejection." TED video, 15:31. Uploaded January 6, 2017. Accessed November 24, 2023. https://youtu.be/-vZXgApsPCQ

3. McLaren, Karla. The Language of Emotions: What Your Feelings Are Trying to Tell You. Boulder: Sounds True, 2010.

4. Betz, Ann. "The Power of Dreaming, the Power of Action." February 6, 2015. Accessed November 24, 2023. https://yourcoachingbrain.wordpress.com/2015/02/06/the-power-of-dreaming-the-power-of-action/

5. Williamson, Marianne. A Return to Love: Reflections On the Principles of A Course in Miracles. New York: HarperCollins, 1996.

6. Lu, Jackson G., Richard E. Nisbett, and Michael W. Morris. "Why East Asians but not South Asians are underrepresented in leadership positions in the United States." Accessed November 24, 2023. https://www.pnas.org/doi/10.1073/pnas.1918896117

7. Erin On Demand. "My life STARTED once I stopped procrastinating! Here's what I did." YouTube video, 13:05. Uploaded August 17, 2023. Accessed November 24, 2023. https://youtu.be/1AUd53dQ_fc

8. Matthews, Gail. "The Harvard Goals Research Summary." Accessed November 24, 2023. https://www.dominican.edu/sites/default/files/2020-02/gailmatthews-harvard-goals-researchsummary.pdf

Chapter Five

1. "Abide." Dictionary.com. Accessed October 15, 2023. https://www. dictionary.com/browse/abide

2. "Kobe Bryant's LAST GREAT INTERVIEW on The MINDSET Of A WINNER & How To SUCCEED." YouTube video, 44:33. Posted by Lewis Howes, September 10, 2018. Accessed October 15, 2023. https://youtu.be/WY0wONSarXA

3. "Experience The Love Meditation Love Is Greater Than Fear During Challenging Times." YouTube video, 6:33. Posted by Kisha Wynter, March 25, 2020. Accessed October 16, 2023. https://youtu. be/THiWz-c9FK4

4. Cascio, Christopher N., Matthew Brook O'Donnell, Francis J. Tinney, Matthew D. Lieberman, Shelley E. Taylor, Victor J. Strecher, and Emily B. Falk. "Self-affirmation activates brain systems associated with self-related processing and reward and is reinforced by future orientation." PLOS ONE 10, no. 11 (2015): e0140857. Accessed January 28, 2024. https://www.ncbi.nlm.nih.gov/pmc/articles/ PMC4814782/pdf/nsv136.pdf

5. Jiang, Jia. Rejection Proof: How I Beat Fear and Became Invincible through 100 Days of Rejection. New York: Harmony Books, 2015.

6. Clear, James. Atomic Habits: An Easy & Proven Way to Build Good Habits & Break Bad Ones. New York: Avery, 2018.

Chapter Six

1. McKinsey & Company. "Women in the Workplace 2016." September 2016. Accessed October 20, 2023. Available at: https://wiw-report. s3.amazonaws.com/Women_in_the_Workplace_2016.pdf

2.   Makoni, Abbianca. "Black And Latinx Employees Face Bias In Job Performance Feedback, Study Finds." People of Color In Tech. July 20, 2022. Accessed October 20, 2023. https://peopleofcolorintech.com/front/black-and-latinx-employees-face-bias-in-job-performance-feedback-study-finds/

3.   McLaren, Karla. The Language of Emotions: What Your Feelings Are Trying to Tell You. Boulder, CO: Sounds True, 2010.

4.   "Paths To Success: Five Career Lessons To Learn From Indra Nooyi." AppleOne Blog. August 7, 2017. Accessed October 21, 2023. https://blog.appleone.com/2017/08/07/paths-to-success-five-career-lessons-to-learn-from-indra-nooyi/

5.   Hewlett, Sylvia Ann. Executive Presence: The Missing Link Between Merit and Success. Sydney, Australia: HarperCollins Publishers Australia Pty Ltd, 2014.

6.   Ibarra, Herminia, Nancy M. Carter, and Christine Silva. "Why Men Still Get More Promotions Than Women." Harvard Business Review, September 2010. Accessed October 21, 2023. https://hbr.org/2010/09/why-men-still-get-more-promotions-than-women

Chapter Seven

1.   Hill, Jemele. "Sherri Shepherd Reflects on 'Very Painful' Years Cohosting The View." https://youtu.be/TAPlwapp1wE, 9:59. Posted by Jemele Hill, March 25, 2020. Accessed May 15, 2023.

2.   Millman, Dan. Way of the Peaceful Warrior: A Book That Changes Lives. Novato, CA: HJ Kramer, 2016.

3.   Leaper, Campbell, and Rachael Robnett. "Women Are More Likely Than Men to Use Tentative Language, Aren't They? A Meta-Analysis Testing for Gender Differences and Moderators." Psychology of Women Quarterly 35, no. 1 (2011): 129-142. doi:10.1177/0361684310392728

4. Hyun, Jane. Breaking the Bamboo Ceiling: Career Strategies for Asians—The Essential Guide to Getting In, Moving Up, and Reaching the Top. New York: Harper Business, 2006.

5. Musselwhite, Chris, and Tammie Plouffe. "What's Your Influencing Style?" Harvard Business Review. Published January 13, 2012. Accessed October 22, 2023. https://hbr.org/2012/01/whats-your-influencing-style.

6. Mohr, Tara. Playing Big: Find Your Voice, Your Mission, Your Message. New York: Gotham Books, 2014.

7. Helgesen, Sally, and Marshall Goldsmith. How Women Rise: Break the 12 Habits Holding You Back from Your Next Raise, Promotion, or Job. New York: Hachette Books, 2018.

8. Mohr, Tara. Playing Big: Find Your Voice, Your Mission, Your Message. New York: Gotham Books, 2014.

Chapter Eight

1. Torres, Monica. "People Are Really, Really Mad About This Viral Salary Advice." Huffpost Post, January 31, 2022. Accessed November 5, 2023. https://www.huffpost.com/entry/recruiter-viral-job-negotiation_l_61f7fbece4b067cbfa201635

2. Ro, Christine. "How the salary 'ask gap' perpetuates unequal pay." BBC. June 18, 2021. Accessed November 5, 2023. https://www.bbc.com/worklife/article/20210615-how-the-salary-ask-gap-perpetuates-unequal-pay

3. Amanatullah, Emily T., and Michael W. Morris. "Negotiating Gender Roles: Gender Differences in Assertive Negotiating Are Mediated by Women's Fear of Backlash and Attenuated When Negotiating on Behalf of Others." February 2010. Accessed November 5, 2023. https://psycnet.apa.org/buy/2010-00584-007

4. Elsesser, Kim. "Women Of Color Set Lower Salary Requirements Than White Men, According to Job Search Site." Forbes, February 6, 2023. Accessed November 5, 2023. https://www.forbes.com/sites/kimelsesser/2023/02/06/women-of-color-set-lower-salary-requirements-than-white-men-according-to-job-search-site/?sh=72803f3a454d

5. Ibid.

6. Kray, Laura, Jessica Kennedy, and Margaret Lee. "Now, Women Do Ask: A Call to Update Beliefs about the Gender Pay Gap." Academy of Management Discoveries. Published online August 15, 2023. https://doi.org/10.5465/amd.2022.0021

7. Watson, Cindy. The Art of Feminine Negotiation: How to Get What You Want from the Boardroom to the Bedroom. New York: Morgan James Publishing, 2023.

8. Rand, Martin. "Women Have Unique Advantages as Negotiators: How Can They Best Leverage Them?" Forbes, March 26, 2021. Accessed November 5, 2023. https://www.forbes.com/sites/martinrand/2021/03/26/women-have-unique-advantages-as-negotiators-how-can-they-best-leverage-them/?sh=7b4325c92dac

9. Mason, Malia F., Alice J. Lee, Elizabeth A. Wiley, and Daniel R. Ames. "Precise offers are potent anchors: Conciliatory counteroffers and attributions of knowledge in negotiations." Journal of Experimental Social Psychology 49, no. 4 (July 2013): 759-763. Accessed November 25, 2023. https://doi.org/10.1016/j.jesp.2013.02.012

Chapter Nine

1. Field, Emily, Alexis Krivkovich, Sandra Kugele, Nicole Robinson, and Lareina Yee. 2023. "Women in the Workplace 2023." McKinsey & Company and Leanin.org, October 5. Accessed

November 11, 2023. https://www.mckinsey.com/featured-insights/diversity-and-inclusion/women-in-the-workplace

2. Ammerman, Colleen, and Boris Groysberg. Glass Half-Broken: Shattering the Barriers That Still Hold Women Back at Work. Boston, MA: Harvard Business Review Press, 2021.

3. Sandberg, Sheryl. Lean In: Women, Work, and the Will to Lead. New York: Alfred A. Knopf, 2013.

4. Wiseman, Liz, Multipliers: How the Best Leaders Make Everyone Smarter. New York: Harper Business, 2017.

5. International Coaching Federation. "All Things Coaching." Accessed November 11, 2023. Available at: https://coachingfederation.org/about

6. Include-Empower.com. "Gender Bias at Work: The Assertiveness Double-Bind." Accessed November 26, 2023. Available at: https://cultureplusconsulting.com/2018/03/10/gender-bias-work-assertiveness-double-bind/

7. Williams, Joan C. "How Women Can Escape the Likability Trap." New York Times, August 16, 2019.

8. Frasca, Teresa J., Emily A. Leskinen, and Leah R. Warner. "Words Like Weapons: Labeling Women as Emotional During a Disagreement Negatively Affects the Perceived Legitimacy of Their Arguments." Sage Journals, vol. 46, no. 4, October 11, 2022. Accessed November 26, 2023. Available at: https://journals.sagepub.com/doi/10.1177/03616843221123745

9. Elsesser, Kim. "Labeling Women As 'Emotional' Undermines Their Credibility, New Study Shows." Forbes, November 1, 2022.

10. Maloney, Mary E., and Patricia Moore. "From aggressive to assertive." International Journal of Women's Dermatology 6, no. 1 (2019):

46-49. doi: 10.1016/j.ijwd.2019.09.006. https://www.ncbi.nlm.nih.gov/pmc/articles/PMC6997833/

11. Elsesser, Kim. "Women More Likely to Negotiate Salaries but Still Earn Less Than Men, Research Says." Forbes, November 2, 2023. https://www.forbes.com/sites/kimelsesser/2023/11/02/women-more-likely-to-negotiate-salaries-but-still-earn-less-than-men-research-says/

12. Ibid.

13. Lean In. "8 Powerful Ways Managers Can Support Equality." Accessed November 26, 2023. Available at: https://leanin.org/tips/managers#!

14. Pino, Ivana. "Understanding the motherhood penalty and what it means for women's finances." Fortune, May 23, 2023. https://fortune.com/recommends/banking/the-motherhood-penalty/

15. Bright Horizons. "Modern Family Index 2018." 2018. Accessed January 27, 2024. https://www.brighthorizons.com/-/media/BH-New/Newsroom/Media-Kit/MFI_2018_Report_FINAL.ashx

16. Gassam Asare, Janice. "How Hair Discrimination Affects Black Women at Work." Harvard Business Review, May 10, 2023. https://hbr.org/2023/05/how-hair-discrimination-affects-black-women-at-work

17. Diehl, Amy, Leanne M. Dzubinski, and Amber L. Stephenson. "Women in Leadership Face Ageism at Every Age." Harvard Business Review, June 16, 2023. https://hbr.org/2023/06/women-in-leadership-face-ageism-at-every-age

18. Tulshyan, Ruchika. "Women of Color Get Asked to Do More 'Office Housework.' Here's How They Can Say No." Harvard Business Review, April 6, 2018. https://hbr.org/2018/04/women-of-color-get-asked-to-do-more-office-housework-heres-how-they-can-say-no

19. Williams, Joan C. and Marina Multhaup. "For Women and Minorities to Get Ahead, Managers Must Assign Work Fairly." Harvard Business Review, March 5, 2018. https://hbr.org/2018/03/

for-women-and-minorities-to-get-ahead-managers-must-assign-work-fairly

20. Cooper, Marianne. "The False Promise of Meritocracy: Managers who believe themselves to be fair and objective judges of ability often overlook women and minorities who are deserving of job offers and pay increases." The Atlantic, December 1, 2015. https://www.theatlantic.com/business/archive/2015/12/meritocracy/418074/

21. Johnson, Stefanie K. Inclusify: The Power of Uniqueness and Belonging to Build Innovative Teams. New York: Harper Business, 2020.

22. Cooper, Marianne. "The False Promise of Meritocracy: Managers who believe themselves to be fair and objective judges of ability often overlook women and minorities who are deserving of job offers and pay increases." The Atlantic, December 1, 2015. https://www.theatlantic.com/business/archive/2015/12/meritocracy/418074/

23. Ibid.

24. Co-Active Training Institute. "The Three Levels of Listening." Co-active Blog, November 30, 2022. Accessed November 27, 2023. https://coactive.com/resources/blogs/levels-of-listening

25. Williams, Joan C. "How Women Can Escape the Likability Trap." New York Times, August 16, 2019.

26. Ibarra, Herminia, and Anne Scoular. "The Leader as Coach: How to Unleash Innovation, Energy, and Commitment." Harvard Business Review, November-December 2019. Accessed November 26, 2023. Available at: https://hbr.org/2019/11/the-leader-as-coach

27. Ammerman, Colleen, and Boris Groysberg, Glass Half-Broken: Shattering the Barriers That Still Hold Women Back at Work. Boston, MA: Harvard Business Review Press, 2021.

28. Ibid.

29. Ibid.

Conclusion: Catching Fire—A Movement, Not a Moment

1. Hanson, Rick. "How to Grow the Good in Your Brain." Greater Good Magazine, September 24, 2013. https://greatergood.berkeley.edu/article/item/how_to_grow_the_good_in_your_brain

Made in the USA
Las Vegas, NV
31 March 2025

20361643R00144